His Majesty Sultan Qaboos bin Said Al-Said

ENCHANTING
OMAN

**Written and photographed
by Shirley Kay**

MOTIVATE
PUBLISHING

Published by
Motivate Publishing
Dubai: PO Box 2331, Dubai, UAE
Tel: (+971 4) 282 4060, fax: (+971 4) 282 0428
e-mail: books@motivate.co.ae   www.booksarabia.com

Office 508, IAA Building (No 8), Dubai Media City, Dubai, UAE
Tel: (+971 4) 390 3550, fax: (+971 4) 390 4845

Abu Dhabi: PO Box 43072, Abu Dhabi, UAE
Tel: (+971 2) 627 1666, fax: (+971 2) 627 1566

London: Acre House, 11/15 William Road, London NW1 3ER
e-mail: motivateuk@motivate.ae

Directors:
Obaid Humaid Al Tayer
Ian Fairservice

© 1988 and 1999 Motivate Publishing

First published 1988
First revised edition 1989
Second revised edition 1992
Reprinted 1994
Fifth printing 1995
Sixth printing 1997
New edition 1999
Reprinted 2001, 2005

ISBN: 1 86063 085 5

British Library Cataloguing-in-Publication Data.
A catalogue record for this book is available from the British Library.

Printed by Emirates Printing Press, Dubai

CONTENTS

Cover: Omani smiles (Photo: Dariush Zandi). Above: The mountains of the Musandam.

Chapter 1

OMAN AND HER PEOPLE

"They are a bold and brave race"
Ibn Batuta, 1329

The very landscape of Oman is dramatic and exciting. Rugged cliffs rise sheer from a deep blue sea; tawny deserts lap up to the foot of arid mountains whose jagged peaks tower high above; deep green palm groves fill a mountain valley or spread out around an ancient mud-built town. Along the plain of the Batinah the palm groves form an uninterrupted belt, and the coastal towns behind them are guarded by ancient forts. In the far south, the mountains of Dhofar turn a lush vivid green with the summer monsoon.

It is the Hajar mountain range, however, that is the backbone of Oman. These mountains have played a central role throughout the history of the land, shaping the character of the people and their destiny. Although the mountains only cover about one-sixth of Oman's total 300,000 square kilometres, they have always dominated the country at their feet, and determined the pattern of settlement there.

THE MOUNTAINS OF OMAN

The Hajar mountains, like the deserts, are remarkable for their aridity. No greenery cloaks their barren rocks and wild contortions. They appear stripped naked, dark and imposing. Strange colours, burnt red, ash grey, green or purple, form sudden abrupt outcrops. To the uninitiated they would seem the result of violent upheavals in some primeval past. This is indeed just what they are. The Hajar mountains were formed some 100 million years ago beneath the ocean to the east, then forced up by huge pressures on to the edge of the continent. Fossil shellfish high up on the Jebel Akhdar, on the high plateau above Sayq, are a witness to this.

A falaj channel carries water along a cliff face of the Jebel Akhdar. Traces of an older falaj are visible above the present one.

7

A falaj surfaces in an old village.

The rocks beneath that ocean so long ago were not all of a kind, however. Some were limestones, a thick bed of solid rock laid down on the ocean floor by ages of sedimentary deposits which hardened with time into the rock layers, clearly visible in the Jebel Akhdar and the Musandam peninsula. Others welled up from beneath the ocean floor, volcanic rocks subjected to immensely high temperatures and colossal pressures as well. These are the rocks of the eastern Hajar, and of the region between the Jebel Akhdar and the Musandam. But nothing here is clear cut; often layers of volcanic rock and layers of limestone are intermingled. At the foot of the Jebel Akhdar are many basalt hills.

The mountains themselves would provide little toehold for mankind, were it not for the luscious greenery in many of the valleys, or *wadis* in Arabic. Here water flows, pink oleanders flower and swaying reeds enliven the scenery. Here was a sheltered haven where palm trees and other crops could be planted on the terraces alongside the *wadi* beds.

But most of the *wadis* are narrow, however, and the scope for cultivation there was limited. When the water from the *wadis* emerged from the mountains it soon ran underground. If agriculture were to be practised on any wider scale it needed a better system of water exploitation; the deep narrow wells which man had sunk into the water table since the days of his earliest settlement in the land were laborious to work before the days of motor pumps.

Great slabs of rock rear up on the flanks of the Jebel Akhdar.

THE FALAJ SYSTEM

The solution to the problem came with the introduction of the ingenious *falaj* system. Some 2,500 years ago or more, the first *falaj* tunnels were dug, running outwards from the foot of the mountains. They were a major engineering feat, underground tunnels sometimes more than a dozen kilometres long, bored under the plain. They were dug by hand, with simple tools, by means of a continuous line of access shafts which look remarkably like a row of bomb craters.

The population of Oman was increasing when the *aflaj* (plural of *falaj*) were first built. Many settlers had come across the narrow strait from Persia and it was almost certainly they who brought with them knowledge of this method of tunnelling for water. Soon they were to be joined by Arab tribes coming from the Yemen, increasing yet further the need for a good water supply.

The first *aflaj* were probably those to the west of the mountains since they are the simplest. A mother well was sunk down to the water table at the foot of the mountains, usually about 20 metres deep but it could go down as far as 60 metres. Another well was then dug some 30 metres away and a tunnel was burrowed out between them, the gradient being just enough for the water to flow down it. Where the tunnel came to the surface, palm groves and a settlement were developed. The *falaj* might also flow for quite a distance above ground. *Falaj* channels hugging the side of the cliffs can be seen in most of the *wadis*, and *aflaj* run like streams through the palm groves and villages.

On the eastern side of the mountains a more complicated technique, the inverted syphon, is sometimes used to bring the *falaj* under a *wadi*. This technique was probably learnt from the Romans, a few hundred years after the first *aflaj* were dug. By the time Islam came to Oman there were some 10,000 *aflaj*, but their number has been decreasing almost ever since.

Nevertheless many *falaj* systems still work today and they are the lifeline of the settlements. Irrigation of this kind was essential, given the often barren terrain. Nearly all the great forts in the country stand on a *falaj*, as do most of the old villages. Unlike modern pumps, they do not exhaust the water supply. The use of *falaj* water is strictly regulated and inherited along with the land. Each farmer has a time share in the *falaj* water, and this is sometimes graphically controlled by a sundial clock, such as the one at Adam where the shadow of a pole falls on metal pegs in the ground. The main use of *falaj* water is to irrigate the palm groves of the great oases near the mountains, or in the valleys. Beneath their shade many other crops can be grown, citrus fruits, mangoes, papaya, bananas, grain and fodder for animals.

Wadi Beni Khalid where perennial water supports lush palm groves.

Although the mountains are a small proportion of the land, most of the population lives within sight of them. The fertile Batinah plain running along the coast is fed by water from the mountains, and the great oasis towns such as Nizwa, Bahla and Rustaq stand at their foot. For the rest, the land consists of extensive deserts.

"A BOLD AND BRAVE RACE"

The population of Oman has increased rapidly in the past few decades, to just over two million in the 1993 census, of whom a little over a quarter were foreigners. With their rapid natural increase of 3.5% a year, Omanis themselves will number two million early in the 21st century. In the past, most people lived in villages or small market towns, but today the capital has developed as a major urban conglomeration with some three quarters of a million people living there. Many still go home to their villages at the weekends though.

Mountain people are frequently tough and independent, and the Omanis are no exception. They learnt from the earliest days to be self-sufficient in their isolated oases and remote *wadis*, and to ensure their own defence. The briefest glimpse of Oman's countryside is more instructive than any history book. Watchtowers on rocky crags guard every palm grove: huge forts defend all the towns, and many villages as well.

Like the other inhabitants of the Arabian Peninsula, the people are grouped into tribes of ancient origin. Some of these tribes came from the Yemen to the south-west, others came from Iraq in the north. All this was a very long time ago but the divisions persisted and sometimes led to strife. In some of the towns the remains of walled districts can still be seen, the homes of different tribes.

Omanis today are a proud and self-confident people, but without the arrogance which sometimes accompanies sudden wealth. A tribute was paid to them in the last century by an English traveller, James Buckingham, who described them as "the cleanest, neatest, best dressed and most gentlemanly of all the Arabs". This innate good taste is still noticeable today. The men wear their headcloths wound in a neat and manly way, the women are a delight in their flowing gowns of exuberant colours, and the whole country is kept refreshingly clean. Along the roadside, even in uninhabited regions, coloured litter bins are provided at regular intervals. Municipal workmen collect up plastic bags and papers alongside the main roads, even in desert areas.

Omanis, too, are extraordinarily hospitable. They are interested in the outside world and will ply the stranger with endless questions about his homeland, then frequently invite him back to their own home for coffee, dates and often a great pile of other fruit as well. Travel slowly in Oman and pause to pass the time of day with anyone who starts up a conversation: it will make your visit all the more enriching.

Of course, Omanis themselves are real travellers, for centuries some of the greatest navigators in the world. They learnt in ancient times to sail on the monsoon winds to India and Africa, and they found their way to China, some 7,000 kilometres away, by about 700 AD. In later centuries they had their own colonies and eventually extensive empire in East Africa, and many Omanis today have spent a part of their lives in Zanzibar. The people of the coastal towns, especially, are outward-looking and of varied origins, some of them Omanis returned from Africa, others of Baluchi or Indian origin but settled for generations in Oman and the main spring of her overseas trade.

Ploughing with oxen is still the most convenient way among the palm trees.

The traditional dagger, the khanjar, is still widely worn at the front of the belt, but today only as a dress ornament.

The prominent Mosque of Asma bint Alawi in Muscat.

Women have always helped with the work of the fields.

A DEVOUT PEOPLE

Omanis are sincerely religious and indeed were one of the first peoples to convert to Islam. In the year 9 AH (Anno Hegirae) the Prophet Muhammad sent his emissary, Amr ibn al As, to convert the leaders and people of Oman, and he remained in the country until the Prophet's death in 11 AH. At that time the Persians still inhabited the land east of the mountains, with their centres at Rustaq and Sohar. The Arab leaders wrote to the Persians, urging them to embrace Islam also, and when the latter refused, attacked them and drove them from the land.

One further obstacle had to be overcome. After the death of the Holy Prophet a number of tribes rebelled, refusing to pay taxes, the Zakat. The Khalif sent armies from Medina to quell this opposition and a great battle was fought on the plain near Dibba. The Khalif's men won and Islam was established firmly in the land for ever more. Strangely, not long after that, a power struggle at the heart of Islam was to affect radically the people of Oman. The Khalif Ali (son-in-law of the Prophet Muhammad) was challenged by Muawiya (founder of the Omayyad dynasty in Damascus) and agreed to submit to arbitration. Some of his followers thought this was wrong, for the Khalif was God's elect; they left his camp and became known as the Kharijites. One group of them came to be called Ibadhis, after their leader Abdullah bin Abadha; a few of these travelled to Oman where their influence soon spread throughout the interior. They advocated return to a pure form of Islam under the direction of an elected leader, the Imam (which means simply 'one who sets an example').

Today the majority of Omanis still follow the Ibadhi teachings, and the Ibadhis are and have always been the main force in Omani politics. Islamic fundamentalism, which takes a different route back to fundamental teachings, has therefore not found fertile ground in Oman and has made little impact here.

Apart from the Ibadhis there are large groups of Sunni Muslims, some of them following the Wahhabi teachings of Saudi Arabia. There are also a number of Shi'a Muslims on the coast, including the Khoja merchants of Muttrah. Some of the Indian merchants are Hindus; and there are also many European and Asian Christian expatriates. Omanis generally are tolerant of others' beliefs. Nevertheless, until quite recently, the Omanis of the interior had little experience of foreigners. Until the late 1950s there were rarely more than 30 Westerners in Muscat and Muttrah, and only the doctor was allowed into the interior. Travellers in Oman today should take care to conform to local customs of suitably conservative dress and behaviour, especially where women are concerned.

WOMEN OF OMAN

In fact women play a more active and visible role in society in Oman than in most of the Arabian Peninsula, where the role of women is still restricted. They have received encouragement and support from the government, which provides schooling and university education for girls on a par with that for boys, and has decreed that women should be given career opportunities and equal pay. In the capital many women now have jobs, especially with the government.

In the countryside women have always played an active role in the agricultural communities. For the most part Omani women are not veiled, although the women of some tribes still wear the *burqa* or face mask and black cloak, the *abaya*. The majority of Omani women, however, wear very colourful clothes arranged in loose and flowing layers. The reds, oranges and ochres of their gowns make a brilliant splash of colour in the old streets of the inland towns and in the fields and palm groves. They are generally not self-effacing and may be willing to talk to strangers, once the ice has been broken. But they are deeply Muslim and should always be treated with deference and respect.

Although the freer, more active role of Omani women has been fostered by the present government, it is not a new phenomenon in Oman. William Palgrave, who visited the coastal areas in the 1860s, was surprised that the families of Sohar practised little segregation of men and women, with no secluded harem area in their homes; "the mutual footing of the sexes is almost European," he commented.

SKILLED CRAFTSMEN

Omanis have a long tradition of skilled craftsmanship, of which traces still survive today. Unfortunately, in any rapidly developing society the role of the crafts is bound to be one of the major losers. It soon becomes so much cheaper, easier and more convenient to buy a colourful plastic bucket in which to carry water, than to make a fine big pot which takes time to produce and is both heavy and breakable. The same goes for many other crafts; cheap rugs from the east become more popular than the beautiful red woven rugs made laboriously by the shepherd people. And the money earned by the craftsmen does not compensate them for the time spent, when they or their sons can command a good wage working for the government. Fortunately examples of Oman's traditional crafts can still be seen today if you search for them, as the following chapters indicate.

One craft which does still seem to flourish, and which must receive a considerable boost from increased tourism,

The women of some tribes still wear the burqa, or face mask, but most are unveiled.

Omani girls are invariably dressed in vibrant colours.

13

A craftsman from Nizwa demonstrates skills in making traditional coffee-pots.

is that of the silversmith. Nizwa in particular has long been known as the source of fine, traditional silver jewellery, and its *souq* is still well stocked with rings, necklaces, bracelets and pendants. Many of these pieces are old and thus irreplaceable. Others are still made in traditional style in the craft *souq*, and in back lanes in the town. Here the tourist may have first choice; Omani women now prefer gold.

In the *souq*, craftsmen also make traditional coffee pots and silver-sheathed *khanjars*. These curved daggers, worn at the front of the belt, were of course in the past workmanlike weapons. Today they no longer have a useful purpose, but have been retained for formal dress wear, and indeed as part of their everyday dress by men of the interior. This continued popularity must be due in large part to the beauty of the scabbard. All *khanjars* are produced with a curved scabbard of woven silver thread, with embossed silver designs on the upper part of the casing, and ornamental silver rings to attach it to the belt. The dagger itself has a handle of bone or rhinoceros horn, partly covered with silver. Dagger handles of the ruling Al Bu Said family are distinguished by a slightly different shape, with a small knob protruding from the top.

A PROFOUND CHANGE

The way of life for Omanis had changed hardly at all over the ages, until the discovery of oil in the 1960s. True, prosperity had fluctuated through the centuries, the best times being linked to the expansion of overseas trade, but wealth only ever came to the few.

There had always been a fairly sharp division, too, between the coastal towns and those of the interior. The towns of the coast were the first to enjoy the results of foreign trade; they suffered less often from inter-tribal strife, being rather set apart, but they were subject every now and then to devastating attacks by foreign powers.

Today the divisions, which often made Oman a series of separate and more or less independent areas, have dissolved in the general wave of prosperity. Development has touched even the remotest areas; motor tracks and concrete houses have reached all but the most physically inaccessible villages. The country is rapidly becoming more homogeneous and her young people all receive a similar schooling. Much of traditional Oman is still there to be explored, but as Oman moves further forward into the modern world, old Oman recedes into the past.

This potter in Bahla throws large water jars on an electric wheel.

Chapter 2

A FRESH START

"A new dawn will rise for Oman and her people"
Sultan Qaboos bin Said Al-Said, 1970

The atmosphere in Muscat was electric in the summer of 1970. Despite the great heat, people were out in the streets in excited groups, quite evidently rejoicing. Bright red banners, the emblem of the Sultan, hung from the roofs and windows of every palm-frond hut, mud-brick cottage, and tall merchant house. Even the town gates and walls were decorated with bright red drapes.

The people were out in the streets to greet the arrival of their Sultan. There was little traffic on any of the roads in those days and the crowds thronged there at ease. This was a very special occasion, for the Sultan of Muscat and Oman had not set foot in his capital for the past 12 years. It was even more special for the people were out to meet their new, young Sultan. His Majesty Sultan Qaboos bin Said Al-Said had just taken power from his father, the elderly Sultan Said bin Taimur Al-Said, who had spent the latter years of his rule cloistered in Salalah in the far south of the country. In July 1970 Qaboos, anxious for his homeland, took over from his father, who abdicated and retired to England.

The Muscat to which Sultan Qaboos came, after spending six years in Salalah at his father's bidding, was like a town from the past, and resembled a place from the Middle Ages. The town was completely surrounded by an ancient wall, pierced by three gateways which were closed at night. Most of the houses within the wall had been built in the prosperous times of the previous century, substantial two-storey houses with high ceilings and light rooms. The *souq* was a huddle of narrow lanes and tiny shops. It was a town with which all visitors fell in love on first sight, but as a modern capital it had its drawbacks.

Access into Muscat was severely limited, being by one small, steep road over the hills from Muttrah. While this had been an advantage when the town was first built,

The timeless beauty of Muttrah's harbour frontage, upon which many maritime traders came to tread.

for it could be easily defended, it was hardly helpful in the days of motor transport. The scope of the town was equally restricted; so small is the bay into which Muscat town is packed that very little extra building could ever be undertaken there. Above all, there was no telephone and no radio by which His Majesty could talk to his new subjects.

The speed with which their new Sultan intended to work was demonstrated to his people within that first week when a radio station was installed and Sultan Qaboos addressed his people. His words were ones of hope: "Oman in the past has been in darkness but, with the help of God, a new dawn will rise for Oman and her people."

A CHALLENGING INHERITANCE

Oman had been a prosperous colonial power in the first half of the 19th century. During the long reign of Sultan Said bin Sultan Al Bu Said, her empire in East Africa was developed to its most profitable extent. Zanzibar especially was the jewel in the crown, producing cloves,

sugar cane and cinnamon, while from Mombassa came ivory and slaves.

The fine merchant houses of Muscat, Muttrah and many small towns in the interior are a legacy of the wealth generated by that trade. Indeed, so important had the African empire become, that in the latter part of his life Sultan Said bin Sultan settled in Zanzibar, just as Sultan Said bin Taimur settled in Salalah a little over a century later.

But when Sultan Said died in 1856, his sons shared his dominions, one taking Oman, the other Zanzibar. The prosperity of Oman collapsed without its African possessions; fairly soon the prosperity of Zanzibar collapsed too without Omani support, and Britain took control of the island in 1890.

Oman now entered a long period of decline and debt which successive Sultans failed to check. In 1932 Sultan Said bin Taimur came to power as a young man of 22, on his father's abdication, and determined seriously to tackle the problem of Oman's growing debts. By measures of strict economy he controlled the deficit and his proudest claim was that "from 1933 until this present day there has been no financial deficit in the government's budget".

Under these circumstances, of course, there was no development either. The people struggled on with a

Drawing up nets on Dibba beach, on the coast of Oman.

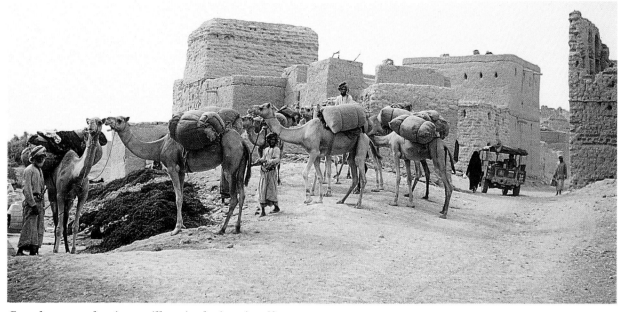
Camel caravan leaving a village in the interior 40 years ago.

subsistence economy, many of them living in extreme poverty. James Morris, who made an epic tour in the interior with the Sultan in 1955, described the people who came to greet them as poor, thin and crippled, bent and pock-marked. And the children, he said, had "such pitiably thin bodies, and such big protruding goggle eyes".

All this is such a far cry from the healthy population of today, and especially from the crowds of energetic children who throng every town and village in Oman, that it would be hard to credit so great a change, had it not been seen within the lifetime of the people.

Deprivation led to disturbances in inner Oman in the 1950s so that Sultan Said, weary of the troubles, retreated in 1958 to Salalah. But it was only a matter of a few years before trouble was brewing near Salalah as well, for in 1965 the Jebel war broke out in Dhofar. Sultan Said was well aware of all that needed to be done for his people, but development had been severely handicapped by lack of funds. When oil revenues started to flow in 1967, he was confronted with a daunting task and had no governmental infrastructure with which to carry it out. Nevertheless some development projects such as new hospitals and a port were started.

An age-old scene at a well in the interior.

RESTRICTIONS

Over the years, too, his fear that Western ways would corrupt his people had led to numerous petty restrictions. The people were not allowed to smoke in the street nor to wear glasses or Western clothes, nor play football. Singing and dancing were banned, men could not move away from their own district without permission, and

Balcony of a fine merchant house on Muttrah Corniche, built in the last century.

Sultan Qaboos University near Seeb.

women had to stay in their village. There was little traffic on the road; to import a car or truck or tractor the Sultan's personal permission had to be sought (about 1,000 vehicles had been imported by 1970, most of them for the army and oil companies).

By 1970 Oman boasted 10 kilometres of asphalted road, from the airport at Bait al Falaj to Muscat, electricity only in Muscat and Muttrah, one hospital established and run by the American mission and five clinics. Most painful of all to the people, perhaps, was the lack of education. There were only three primary schools in the

country (in Muscat, Muttrah and Salalah with some 900 boys attending). Other teaching was provided by the Koran schools; a group of children, both boys and girls, gathered beneath a shady tree to learn to read and recite the Koran, taught by a religious old man.

Those seeking education at a level higher than primary had to go abroad to find it, and once they had acquired higher education they did not return home. In 1970 there were no Omani graduates in the country although many were working elsewhere in the Gulf. Altogether some 50,000 Omanis were thought to be working abroad at that time.

THE NEW DAWN

The extent of the achievement of HM Sultan Qaboos can only be appreciated against the background of the country as it was in 1970. Prosperity has spread throughout the land; the country has been bound together by an ever-expanding network of highways, and by participation in government employment. Such cohesion had rarely been known throughout the country's history. The very name of 'Muscat and Oman' was divisive and was rapidly replaced by 'the Sultanate of Oman'.

Oman's income from oil is not large, far smaller than that of most of its neighbours in the Arabian Peninsula, while its land area is relatively extensive, the second biggest in the peninsula. Whenever the oil has seemed about to run out, however, more has been found, and the

Village boys returning home from school.

income from it has been spent swiftly and effectively on developing the basic infrastructure.

A few statistics can illustrate the extent of the change: by the late 1990s Oman had 6,000 kilometres of asphalted roads (compared with 10 kilometres in 1970). There are now 47 hospitals (two small ones in 1970), 114 health centres and five extended health centres; vaccination and preventative medicine have been spread throughout the country and average life expectancy has soared from 49 years in 1970 to over 71 today.

The effects of this medical care are striking: whereas in the past infant mortality was high and the children frequently sickly looking (as James Morris recorded), the country now is alive with children. They are indeed the most lasting impression that one carries away of Oman today, children laughing and playing everywhere,

Giant cranes at Mina Qaboos, Muttrah, challenge the rocky heights of the surrounding mountains.

Chapter 3

MUSCAT, THE CAPITAL

"Muscat is a port, the like of which cannot be found in the whole world, where there are merchants and all ships aim for it."
Ahmad ibn Majid, 1490

Muscat has been the capital of Oman for more than two centuries, since the third Al Bu Said ruler established his residence there in the 1780s. Until 1970 its name was woven into that of the country, 'Muscat and Oman'. A name with so much fame, one feels, should belong to a sizeable place. Yet the old town of Muscat is less than a kilometre long by half a kilometre wide. It is no less impressive for all that: an unforgettable little gem of a place tightly enclosed in its rocky bay by barren, brown-black mountains. And the bay itself is as picturesque as the town, a horseshoe of deep-blue water surrounded by rocky promontories and islets, all but hidden from the open sea. "There was something soothing and magical about that old city at night", wrote James Morris 40 years ago.

Muscat had been a flourishing port since the beginning of Islam. In the 16th century AD it was taken by the Portuguese commander, Alfonso de Albuquerque, who described it thus: "Muscat is a very large, populous town (by 16th century standards of course), with fine elegant houses, flanked on both sides with high mountains." The Portuguese, who were to hold Muscat for 150 years, made the natural harbour more secure by constructing a pair of massive fortresses perched on the rocks on either side of the bay, the forts of Merani and Jalali, completed in 1587/88. Today, carefully renovated, they are picture-book forts, giving the town a fairy-tale appearance. They were major strongholds, however, and their strength is echoed by the watchtowers crowning the hills around the town.

Muscat is one of the world's most romantic capitals.

The decorative tiling of a minaret gleams beneath the sombre Fort Merani.

The Sultan's Palace in Muscat is reminiscent of a fairy-tale residence of exotic style and colours.

A NATURAL STRONGHOLD

From the land side, too, Muscat was a natural stronghold. In the past the only way into the bay was over precipitous little donkey tracks, each guarded by a watch-tower. The first road in, a very steep one, was cut over the hill from Riyam on the Muttrah side in 1929. This old road still exists and is worth taking for one of the best views over Muscat, from the top. Recently a wide corniche road was built from Muttrah, and another road to the south, down past the fishing village of Sidab.

Until 1970, however, the Riyam road was the only way into the capital, and indeed the only asphalted road in the Sultanate. It led from the city's airport at Bait al Falaj, a nerve-wracking place in which to land, for the mountains seemed about to snag the plane's wing tips on either side. This solitary road led past Muttrah, over the hill and down to the city walls of Muscat. These old walls, now replaced with a new version, enclosed the town completely and their gates were shut three hours after sunset. Within the walls those who ventured into the streets at night had to carry a paraffin lantern, a *butti* as it was called.

Once inside the walls, the surfaced road divided, one branch leading to the palace beneath Fort Merani, the other to the British Consulate General beneath Fort Jalali. For the rest the town was a maze of narrow sandy lanes, so quiet that animals could safely share them with humans; an ostrich was recorded as a pet there in 1920, and in 1970 a tame gazelle still roamed at liberty.

Today all that has changed. The *souq* with its narrow sandy lanes has given way to large government buildings and asphalted roads; the gates are always open. Muscat has remained a quiet place, however, enclosed in its secretive bay. The Sultan's Palace, built in the early 1970s, occupies a third of the seafront, its lawn projecting out into the bay. But life seems to have drained from Muscat to the north-west, via the larger town of Muttrah into the modern suburbs of Ruwi, Qurum, Madinat Qaboos etc and out as far as Seeb, with its new international airport, some 35 kilometres away.

A few of the fine old merchant houses within the walls have been preserved and renovated. One of the best of them, Bait Nadir, has served as a museum: and Bait Zawawi was for a time the American Embassy. The old British Embassy building on the seafront was demolished

27

A window of old Muscat.

SIDAB AND BUSTAN

A new road runs over the rocky ridge to the south of Muscat and immediately drops down into the delightful bay of Sidab. A fishing village fills this bay and its beach is always alive with fishermen and their boats, pulled up out of the water. The road runs between the houses and the beach which is the centre of life for the village, both in terms of livelihood and community spirit.

Beyond Sidab is another little fishing village and then a couple more small bays, the latter of which, Rawdah, houses Fisheries Research Centre. On the beach beside this centre are the remains of a 17th century fort.

The road then climbs another ridge and suddenly, below, Al Bustan bay curves away to the mountain wall enclosing it. A model fishing village of pleasant white houses has been built on the golden beach at the northern end of the bay, to replace an old village a little further along. Close to its old site now stands the magnificent Al Bustan Palace Hotel, sharply outlined against the black mountains behind. Fishermen mend nets on the beach and their children sell bundles of jasmine wrapped in large green leaves. The famous *dhow*, the Sohar, which recently made the journey to China, has come to rest on a roundabout at the road junction there.

in 1996. Perhaps the most celebrated of these houses, the Bait Fransa, home of the first French consul and of some well-known writers, has become a Franco-Omani museum. These large white houses with their long narrow rooms grouped around a central courtyard preserve a cool interior, and evoke an atmosphere of quiet elegance.

The model fishing village of Al Bustan Bay.

The Al Bustan Hotel was the jewel in the crown for the first GCC convention held in Muscat in 1985.

MUTTRAH

Muttrah is Muscat's twin town on a bay only four kilometres to the west. It was always the bigger of the two, for its bay is wider and has better access to the interior. In the 1950s, Muttrah was described as the largest town in the land (its population estimated at 8,000, compared with Muscat's 5,000). Since then Oman's population has increased and has become far more urban. At the end of 1998, the population of the whole capital area had reached some three quarters of a million.

Muttrah has changed to keep pace with this development and the major change here is, so to speak, offshore, rather than on land. A large part of Muttrah's bay has been filled with the modern harbour of Mina Qaboos, completed in 1974. Colourful piles of container cargoes line its wharves and giant cranes point skywards behind the *dhows* and fishing boats at anchor in the bay.

The seafront has changed too. The fine old merchant houses with ornate balconies, which line the corniche's dual carriageway, once stood directly on the beach. Only a few survive, however; more than half the bay is now fronted with modern buildings. Behind the old houses is a district closed to outsiders, whose narrow lanes and old buildings have scarcely been touched by modern development, a district inhabited by traders of Indian origin, the Khojas. Close beside it, the colourful narrow lanes of the old *souq* are still as busy as ever, selling traditional silver, spices, textiles from the East, plastic bowls and buckets, leaf tobacco, bright cotton *dishdashas*, and sticky sweet *helwa* mixed in great cauldrons in some of the back lanes. The main lanes were upgraded in 1997, with new roofing and paving.

THE NEW CITY

The dual carriageway sweeps inland from Muttrah to Ruwi where once stood the old customs post which levied taxes on all goods coming from the interior. Today Ruwi is the heart of the modern business district; high-rise buildings, banks, the Ministry of Commerce, and modern hotels are all sited there.

The old Bait al Falaj airport ran along the wadi here, and near it still stands the fort which was once a military headquarters. This *wadi* has now been opened up by a huge cutting through the mountain to the south-east, carrying a highway through the Wadi Kabir down to Al Bustan bay on the far side of Muscat.

Facing Ruwi, to the north, stands the hilly promontory of Qurum. This was the only other area with any substantial development prior to 1970, for it was the place chosen by the oil company, Petroleum Development Oman or PDO, for their oil terminal and refinery of Mina al Fahal. It was a good site, for Qurum is the last rocky outcrop on the seashore before the long coastal plain of the Batinah flattens the coast line all the way from here to the frontiers of the UAE.

At the foot of the Qurum outcrop is a large creek, the mouth of the Wadi Adai. This area is now a nature reserve, for the mangrove trees which line the creek are a natural haven for birds and other wildlife. They also attracted fishermen thousands of years ago; their ancient camps have been excavated on the cliffs above. The district itself takes its name from the mangrove trees, *Qurum* in Arabic. A large public park nearby has a popular heritage centre with demonstrations of traditional crafts.

Westwards from Qurum the plain between the mountains and the sea has been developed with large residential districts all the way to Seeb airport. A six-lane dual carriageway lined with trees and shrubs takes traffic rapidly all the way from Muttrah to Seeb, thanks to numerous flyovers and an impressive rock cutting near Qurum. The contrast with the same area in 1970 is dramatic. Then this plain was uninhabited apart from a few fisher folk who pulled up their high-sterned fishing boats on the beach. The few motorists who made the journey preferred to drive along that beach if the tide was out, scattering

hundreds of crabs as they went. It was easier than the bumpy track over the plain.

Such rapid development might have produced a characterless town, a hotchpotch of disparate buildings. Fortunately this has not been the case. There is a surprising homogeneity in the new capital, and developers are encouraged to incorporate traditional Omani features such as arches, crenellations, walls sloping slightly inwards, and so on. Districts are spaciously laid out, delightfully clean, and gardens are now producing a blaze of colour. Among the large number of new villas built over the last few years, many are of pleasing design.

Above all there are now some buildings of genuine architectural distinction, especially those commissioned by the government such as the new ministries, hospitals and university. Sited alongside the motorway out to Seeb, the line of new ministries, each one quite different in design yet harmonious in style, make a particular impact. These buildings were completed before the AGCC meeting in Muscat in 1985, along with the main development of the road which they front. They are almost more impressive at night, thanks to attractive floodlighting. Further out, the vast Sultan Qaboos mosque was built in the Bawsher district in the late 1990s.

The imposing pink façade of the Centre for Investment and Export Development in Muscat.

Just beyond the airport the village of Seeb has become a pleasant little country town. It is virtually a garden suburb, for here are large numbers of country properties with fine houses surrounded by spacious and shady gardens, built close to the beach.

Although a little place, Seeb has its page in the history books, thanks to the Treaty of Seeb, signed there in 1920. By this treaty the duty charged on goods from the interior at the Ruwi customs post was limited to five per cent, free access to the markets of Muscat and Muttrah was assured to the tribesmen and the Sultan guaranteed not to interfere in tribal affairs; the tribes, in their turn, pledged to live at peace with the people of the coast.

The elegant new Ministry of Foreign Affairs building.

NEIGHBOURING DISTRICTS

Surprisingly, just a few kilometres inland of all this dynamic modern development, is the old traditional village of Bawsher, a village not yet transformed by the modern Oman. Here you can wander along sandy lanes beneath palm trees, alongside a sparkling *falaj* where women still wash their clothes and little boys swim. A renovated mud fort dominates the *falaj* and there are some nice, arched buildings. In the neighbouring village of Fateh stands another impressive fort, also beside a *falaj* equipped with new concrete bathing places. On the hills and along the plain near Bawsher a number of ancient burial mounds have been excavated.

A few kilometres inland also, but rather further out of town, is Oman's new university. It has been built in a bowl among the hills, a little to the west of the Seeb-Nizwa road. The university is the jewel in the crown of the Sultanate's educational system which has been developed almost in its entirety since 1970. The university concentrates largely on the sciences and especially on medicine (it has its own hospital); there are also faculties of Education and Islamic Sciences, Agriculture, Engineering, Science, Arts, Commerce and Economics.

The design of the campus is very appealing, with long shaded cloisters leading from one section to another. Men and women students have separate boarding houses but share lectures although they approach by cloisters at different levels. Women students are now strongly in the majority, since men are more likely to study abroad.

Just inland of the university is the capital's industrial district of Rusail, at the foot of the mountains. A power station and gas plant are located here, along with many other private industrial developments, in a spacious site which is conveniently close to the capital, yet far enough away not to impinge on its amenities.

Oman's coast offers the perfect relaxing holiday destination for all the family.

Youngsters of Bawsher receive a good state education.

Chapter 4

THE SEA COAST

"Whenever a vessel arrives at their town they show the greatest joy."
Ibn Batuta, 1329

Oman has a very long shoreline. Some 1,700 kilometres of sea coast border the Indian Ocean, the Gulf of Oman, and curl round the Strait of Hormuz into the Arabian Gulf. The coast varies from near vertical cliffs in the Musandam and south of Muscat, to the low flat shores of the Batinah plain north of the capital. But everywhere it has one factor in common, the magnificently rich fisheries of the warm seas, close inshore.

Omani fishermen bring in between 120,000 and 160,000 tonnes of fish a year and some 25,000 men are employed in fishing. The government has taken steps to control over-fishing, aided by the Marine and Science Fisheries Centre near Sidab, south of Muscat. The government also helps by supplying outboard motors and aluminium or fibreglass boats at subsidised rates; these have all but replaced the traditional high-sterned *badans*, palm-frond *shashas* and dugout canoes, or *houris*. Some larger *dhows* are still built though, and many can be seen in the harbours along the coast.

THE BATINAH

The extensive plain of the Batinah runs between the sea and the mountains for 270 kilometres from the frontier with the UAE south-east to Muscat. Its width varies, averaging about 25 kilometres, and it is one of the most densely inhabited regions in the Sultanate, with over half a million inhabitants. Along the highway it seems the plain is continuously built up, almost for its entire length.

The tranquil village of Ayga across the water from Sur, whose enduring maritime livelihood is etched in the simply sculpted mud-brick lighthouse.

Sohar's whitewashed dwellings beneath the jagged parapet of the town's fort.

This is rather misleading, however. The cultivation, and hence the villages, are all concentrated in a three to five kilometre-wide strip along the coast, where their inhabitants enjoy a double income, from sea and land. About half of Oman's cultivated land is in the Batinah.

The palm groves are densely green, sheltering limes, bananas, pomegranates, figs, papaya, mangoes, guavas and a selection of vegetables beside. Limes are still a major export and dried limes can be bought in all the *souqs*. Indian roller birds add a vivid splash of colour to the groves, and older men still jog along the quiet lanes on camels and donkeys.

Modern life has swept through the Batinah along the motorway. Although recent accounts of the plain describe palm-frond huts as commonplace, today the road is lined with new concrete houses. For a while, the only real *barasti* was the government-run weaving and develop-

ment centre near Khabura. There a large group of women learnt reading and writing, as well as traditional ground-loom weaving. "My mother wove in just the same way" claimed one woman. Today the centre has expanded to a modern concrete building in which the traditional craft thrives. The government buys the woven trappings for animals and the narrow rugs that are produced there.

Since cultivated fields alternate with patches of acacia-studded desert, it seems that the whole of the Batinah might be farmed. The constraint, of course, is water. The Batinah is one of the most fortunate regions in the land, with a good water table fanning out from the mountains; as it approaches the sea the water rises near the surface and can be tapped by wells, or augmented by *falaj* systems. But a well is simpler to make than a *falaj* and in recent times, with diesel pumps, the ground water has been over-exploited and is becoming saline as a result.

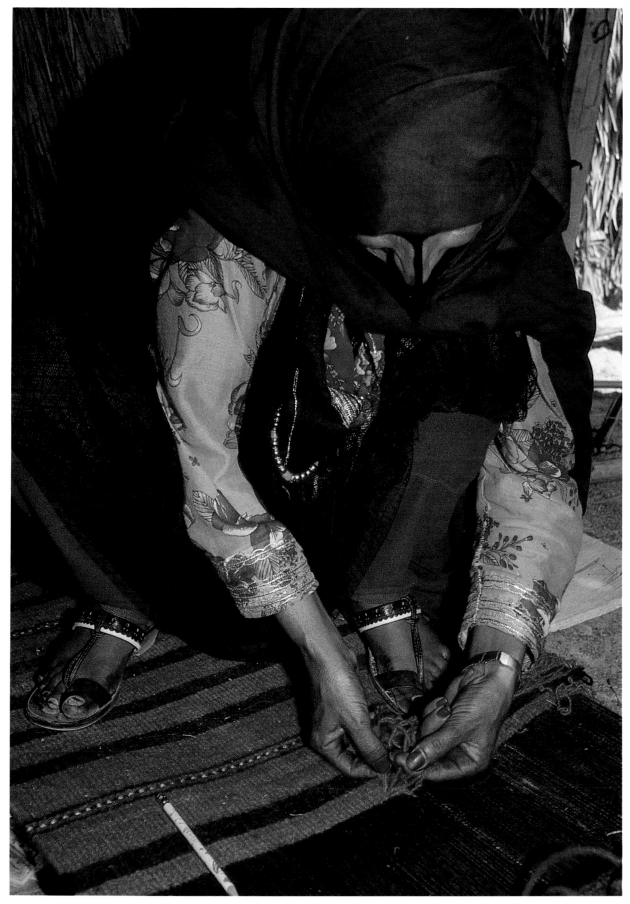

Working on a ground loom at the government-sponsored weaving centre near Khabura.

Now the Ministry of the Environment is taking control of water exploitation in the region; a number of recharge dams have been built to prevent occasional floods rushing wasted to the sea.

The *falaj* systems, which drew water from further inland in the mountains, have for the most part fallen into ruin. Inland of Sohar, the major town of the Batinah, 23 *aflaj* have been found but only two of them still work today. One of the ancient *aflaj* brought water from 36 kilometres away in the Wadi Jizzi, to supply the palm groves and citizens of the town.

SOHAR

Sohar stands at the mouth of the great Wadi Jizzi, a major route through the northern mountains. Near the coast no *wadi* can be seen, however, only a series of shallow depressions crossing the road, and a delightful area of shady *ghaf* trees inland of the palm belt. But on the shore the waters must have been channelled through creeks on either side of the ancient town. Both creeks are now very small and silted. The wadi can still show its force, however: in a freak storm early in 1988 floods tore down the creeks, destroying the coast road and several houses.

Today one approaches through extensive suburbs of new villas under shady *ghaf* trees, through palm groves no more impressive than those of other villages, to where the old town stood on its raised mound between the two creeks. But here little is left to recall the past. In the 1990s modern villas replaced the old *souq* and houses built of small, rounded red bricks, originally baked in the kilns of 10th century Sohar and reused continuously ever since.

The most impressive building is the great fort beside the sea from which it is now separated by a recent police post, wali's office and corniche road. Its walls and towers painted white, loom above a moat cut into the mound of the old city, and the square central keep dominates a fine view of the town. In the courtyard excavations have revealed the foundations of an earlier brick-built fort of the 14th century. The keep, in which one ruler was murdered in the 19th century, has now been turned into a small museum showing objects from Sohar's past.

The fort and former old town were built on a tell, a low hill made up of the debris of the houses of previous towns. Sohar is one of Oman's most ancient and famous cities, although at first glance there is little to suggest as much today. Its history is well recorded too, since Sohar stands on the coast and was visited by many perceptive travellers in the past.

Sohar was already a substantial town before Islam. It was the capital of the Persians then. They were driven out of Sohar in the early years of Islam, but attacked the town again in later centuries. Their final attack was foiled in

The fort at Sohar has been rebuilt many times. It stands on a mound beside the beach.

The strange rock shape at Lasail copper mine is close beside the ancient mine shaft.

1748 by the first of the Al Bu Said rulers. Sohar always attracted outsiders; it was taken several times over by the Portuguese in the 16th and early 17th centuries.

It was the early Islamic city of Sohar, however, that reached the height of its prosperity and fame. In the ninth and tenth centuries AD it was a leading port, described by the 10th century writer Al Muqaddasi as a city of 12,000 houses, "the hallway to China, the store house of the East". Small wonder that it is alleged to be the home town of Sindbad the Sailor. Other 10th century Arab geographers wrote in the same vein. Istakhri said, "It is not possible to find on the shore of the Persian Sea nor in all the land of Islam a city more rich in fine buildings and foreign wares than Sohar", and Ibn Hawqal added, "Its traders and commerce cannot be enumerated".

In those days the palm groves covered an area of over 60 square kilometres and the town boasted a copper smelting industry and baked-brick kilns. But the city was sacked twice in the late 10th century and never really recovered.

COPPER OF MAGAN

The prosperity of Sohar was supported by a key export, copper. In the strange, almost lunar, volcanic foot-hills of the Wadi Jizzi, copper had been discovered long ago, more than 3,000 years before Sohar's greatest days in fact. Copper was exported from there in early times, to the Sumerians of ancient Mesopotamia (now Iraq). Copper was the most valuable mineral to control, and the deposits in the Hajar mountains brought considerable wealth to Oman during the Bronze and Iron Ages. Driving up the Wadi Jizzi from Sohar you see strange bumps along the ridges of the hills, the burial mounds of the past. Further up the Wadi, nearer Buraimi, the furnaces of an ancient copper smelter have been restored. They are surrounded by piles of slag.

In the 1980s the state-owned Oman Mining Company reopened the ancient copper mines of the Wadi Jizzi and by the middle of the decade was exporting yearly almost 15,000 tonnes of refined copper cathodes to Britain, the Far East, and the Gulf states. These mines were reworked from 1983 to 1994 and produced over 141,000 tonnes of copper cathode. Further large deposits of copper have now been found along the Batinah and in the Yanqul area near Ibri.

In reworking the old mining areas, many traces of former miners were found, the earliest going back nearly 4,500 years. Lasail was the largest old mine in the Wadi Jizzi. There are 100,000 tonnes of ancient slag there, and a large opencast mining pit.

Beside the pit is a man-made rock arch, which has a twin in another ancient mine, but its purpose is unknown. The modern mine shaft at Lasail cut across early Islamic mine workings down to a depth of 87 metres. The ancient miners worked in tunnels less than a metre high and just over half a metre wide.

The mausoleum of Bibi Miriam alone survives among the ruins of Qalhat.

A Sohar fisherman with a traditional boat.

MUSCAT TO RAS AL HADD

Near the capital the mountains draw into the sea and from Muscat southwards steep brown-black cliffs drop sheer to the water or enclose secluded sandy bays. An occasional ridge of sandstone, like the bay of Bandar Jisah near Muscat, provides a welcome, golden relief from this dark backdrop.

Here and there a *wadi* cuts its way to the sea, enclosing a sheltered creek at its mouth, and at such sites the ancient ports of this stretch of coast have been built. Like the ports of the Batinah, these towns too were much visited in the past, by friend and foe. Their fortunes fluctuated between periods of surprising prosperity, partly based on the yet more surprising export of horses, and disaster wrought by invaders. Today, of the three major towns of this coast in former times, one is still a flourishing port, another a fishing village, and the third a mass of ruins. A diving centre now exploits this magnificent stretch of coastline.

Qurayyat, the nearest town to Muscat, stands at the northern end of a plain surrounded by mountains; herds of fine horses once grazed on the plain, though none are to be seen today. Qurayyat is little more than a village now, with a small souq, a white-washed fort, and a watchtower on a little rocky islet just offshore as the only reminder of more impressive times. Its creek has silted and the place was utterly demoralised in 1506, when many of its inhabitants were massacred by Portuguese attackers for having put up the stiffest resistance on the coast.

Qalhat, some 80 kilometres south of Qurayyat, and linked by a good graded track, has met a far more dramatic fate. Today the high bluff between mountains and sea which once was an imposing city is but a pile of ruins, shattered stone walls, empty cisterns, broken tombs. Only one building of any size is left standing and that is the mausoleum of Bibi Miriam, standing alone on the highest ridge. An outer and an inner city wall of considerable strength still stand a metre high, running from the mountain to the sea, while the remains of a massive tower lean broken on the beach at the end of the inner wall.

A deep *wadi* runs out of the mountains on the northern side of the bluff. It still has a little water at its mouth but is for the most part now filled with gravel. On the far side of the *wadi* stands a small modern village, a pale reflection of the once great city above. An early description of Qalhat was given by Marco Polo in the 13th century: "This city has a very good port, much frequented by merchant ships from India. Many fine horses are exported from here to India... the total number of horses shipped to India from this port and the others I have mentioned is past all reckoning."

A man of the sea coast near Qurayyat.

Erosion by the sea caused spectacular overhanging of the rock above.

Waiting for the ferry from Sur to Ayga.

A few decades later the Arab geographer, Ibn Batuta, paid a painful visit to the town. He landed at Sur in 1329 AD and was told that Qalhat was "just down the road"; a hot 20 kilometres walk further on, he finally reached his goal, and was impressed: "The town of Qalhat lies on the shore: it has fine bazaars and an exceedingly beautiful mosque, the walls of which are decorated with Qashani tile work... the inhabitants are traders and live entirely on what comes to them from the Indian Ocean. Whenever a vessel arrives at their town they show the greatest joy."

But Qalhat suffered the same fate as Qurayyat. In 1508 it was sacked by the Portuguese but perhaps it was already declining. Albuquerque, commander of the Portuguese fleet described it thus: "Calayate is a city as large as Santarem, badly populated, with many old edifices now destroyed. This port is a great entrepot for shipping which comes thither to take horses and dates to India." The destruction of the Portuguese was reinforced by that of an earthquake, the creek silted and the city never recovered.

Had Ibn Batuta walked from the thriving port of Sur to Qalhat today, he would have come across Oman's largest development project, just before the ridge of mountains drop down to the sea. Here a vast LNG (liquefied natural gas) plant was built on the shore in the late 1990s, to process huge reserves of gas discovered in central Oman at the beginning of the decade. The project should ensure Oman's prosperity for the next half century.

SUR

The extensive town of Sur seems to have emerged from the doldrums into which it had sunk until the 1970s. Modern houses now spread right across its promontory to the north of the creek at the mouth of the Wadi Fulaij. It is here that Sur has been fortunate, for this long curving creek is still open and active, a haven for *dhows* many of which are still built along its banks.

Sur is an ancient town but in the past was surpassed by neighbouring Qalhat. After the decline of that port, however, it came into its own as the main centre for trade with Oman's expanding empire in East Africa. Merchant families there, and in the towns directly inland, made their fortunes on the trade in slaves and cloves. Houses with fine carved doors, and decorative panels above the windows, were built among the palm groves of Sur, where many still stand today. But trade with East Africa declined after the middle of the last century, and Sur's fortunes declined too.

In its heyday Sur had been one of the greatest of Oman's shipyards and even today numerous fishing *dhows* are still being built or repaired there. It was here, in 1980, that Tim Severin chose to construct his traditional *dhow* with sewn planks for his epic voyage to China. But he named the *dhow* Sohar after that chief port of the China trade.

Beside Sur's *dhow* yard a ferry carries passengers across the creek to the still unchanged village of Ayga, built directly on the beach opposite. Ayga is the port of the Beni Bu Ali tribe whose centre lies inland at Bilad Beni Bu Ali, on the edge of the Wahiba Sands. A murder here in 1820 brought down the wrath of the British Empire.

Some 25 kilometres east of Sur is the cape of Ras Al Hadd, the most easterly point of the Arabian Peninsula which is located at the dividing line between the Indian Ocean and the Gulf of Oman. Men settled here over 4,000 years ago, on a steep bluff above the beach where archaeologists are at present uncovering their settlement and graves.

A female turtle returning to the sea after laying hundreds of eggs.

They were probably attracted by the shore's other denizens, the green turtles which painfully plough their way up the beach at night to dig the holes in which they lay their hundreds of white eggs. Weeks later the tiny turtles hatch all at once and scramble wildly down to the sea, where distressingly few of them will survive to adulthood. Five species of turtles frequent Oman's coast today and the breeding grounds here and on Masirah island are the largest known in the world. They are protected, for turtles are becoming an increasingly endangered species.

Sur's shipyard is appropriately located on the creek.

Chapter 5

FORTIFIED TOWNS OF THE JEBEL AKHDAR

"A fertile land with streams, trees, orchards, palm gardens, and fruit trees of various kinds. "
Ibn Batuta, 1329

The Jebel Akhdar, at the centre of the Hajar mountain range, is the very heart of Oman. Its great bulk looms more than 3,000 metres above the surrounding plain, with huge slabs of grey limestone tilted upwards at a vertiginous angle around its flanks. Nowhere could one see more clearly the effects of massive geological upheavals in primeval times, for these vast flanking slabs were once sections of the earth's crust deep down below the ocean.

One of the clearest places to see this strange geological formation is along the quiet Wadi Ghul, at the southern foot of the mountain. At the entrance to the *wadi*, the attractive village of Al Hamra is built on sloping rock, its fine mud houses adapted to the incline and its rocky lanes polished with wear.

Further down the *wadi* is the yet more spectacular village of Ghul. Here the old mud-built village was perched on an extremely steeply sloping slab, the oldest village highest up, a more recent version below it. A steep cliff drops from the village to the *wadi* floor where green fields are still cultivated, and from where all the village's water had to be carried. Palm groves run along the side of a steep gorge which cuts into the mountain behind the rock slab on which the old village is perched. A new village has been built on a slightly lower cliff, on the opposite side of this gorge.

Patches of cultivation are to be found right up to a height of 2,000 metres on the Jebel, but this can scarcely justify its name of 'The Green Mountain'. True, the high plateau is dotted with juniper bushes and small shrubs in a

The great fort of Nakhl, renovated and restored.

Great gorges cut into the flanks of the Jebel with terraced villages clinging to their cliffs.

dry stony setting reminiscent of Mediterranean shores, but even there, in that cool clear air above, the effect could hardly be described as green. Only near the villages around the high plateau is the mountain really green.

There, terraced fields support luxuriant crops of walnuts, peaches, figs, limes, pomegranates, grapes and roses, while maize, barley, vegetables and lucerne grow on other terraces.

The mud-brick villages cling to the steep slopes; on the flat roofs of the houses limes and maize are spread out to dry. In the past, life at the top was harsh; the climb up along donkey paths, made only a little easier by ancient steps cut in the rock, would take some six hours. Today Sayq, the main village at the top, has a school and hospital, and water is delivered regularly to large metal tanks in the village square. A graded road of dizzying steepness has been constructed all the way up to Sayq; it is a military road and permission is required to use it.

This new road starts at the village of Birkat Al Mauz, traditionally a gateway to the Jebel. Here a narrow gorge leads into the mountains, guarded by a mud-brick fort at the entrance. Until it was renovated in 1990, the fort stood in ruins, destroyed in the fighting around the Jebel in the 1950s. It belonged then to Sulaiman bin Himyar, sheikh of the powerful Beni Riyam tribe and 'Lord of the Green Mountain'; Thesiger, to whom he refused passageway, judged him "an autocrat accustomed to obedience."

When, in 1954, the newly elected Imam, Ghalib Al Hina'i and his brother Talib rebelled against the Sultan, Sulaiman joined them. But gradually they were driven back and took refuge on the Jebel Akhdar. The jebel was a natural redoubt and had only once been taken by force, by a Persian army in 973 AD. So the Sultan called on British help and in early 1959 the SAS and Sultan's forces stormed the mountain at night, bringing the rebellion to an end.

Sulaiman's other major stronghold, and headquarters, was the village of Tanuf, also at the entry to a gorge leading into the mountains some 20 kilometres west of Birkat Al Mauz. Tanuf too was destroyed by rockets during the rebellion; today its ruined mud-built houses stand attractively on a ridge of rock concealing the entrance to the gorge behind. But the magnificent *falaj*, built on a ledge along the side of the gorge, still runs through the old village and out to the palm groves. A huge new dam has now been built further up the gorge.

Modern industry was attracted to Tanuf by the reputation of its *falaj* water, said to be of particular sweetness. A mineral water bottling plant was installed there in 1979, drawing its water from wells at the mouth of the gorge. Tanuf bottled water now supplies half the Omani market and the plant produces about 600,000 bottles a month. Half the factory's employees are local people who still cultivate their palm groves, after work.

A woman's colourful dress enlivens an old archway in Nizwa.

FORTRESSES SOUTH OF THE JEBEL

Nizwa is the major town on the south side of the Jebel. In the past it was always important even when the capital was moved elsewhere. An asphalt road linking it with Muscat was completed in 1976 and made into a dual carriageway in the late 1990s.

The town lies along a *wadi* and does not appear to have a particularly strategic location. It has good water supplies, however, from the *wadi* and from the prolific Falaj Daris. Extensive palm groves line the wadi on either side, providing a pleasantly green and shady setting for the old mud-built houses. In the past Nizwa was divided into several districts and the remains of enclosure walls and defensive towers can still be seen.

Nizwa is very ancient and was the capital of the Julanda dynasty in the 6th and 7th centuries AD. They received a highly significant visit in the early years of Islam, when Amr ibn al As, emissary of the Prophet Muhammad, visited the town in 630 AD (9 AH) and converted the Julanda rulers. They then seized control of the

a gun, dagger or copper bowl. Just outside this *souq*, a fruit and vegetable market is held in an open space beneath a palm tree.

In one of the little lanes off the *souq* a metal worker fashions his products over a fire in the centre of his shop. Further along, Bahla's remaining indigo dyer is at work. He has a tiny shop, in the side of which is the pot in which he mixes his indigo and steeps dresses, veils, masks and lengths of cloth in the blue black dye. Then he hangs them from the roof of his shop to dry. He is the descendant of a long line of indigo dyers and intends to continue his craft. The indigo comes from a plant which looks rather like blue alfalfa. Omani indigo is processed into little flat plaques whose colour, he claims, is fast. Indigo from abroad comes in powder form and the colour may run.

Bahla has preserved another of its ancient crafts, that of the potter. To encourage local people to continue this craft the government has established a pottery by the roadside at the entrance to the town, with Chinese advisers. The old traditional pottery still flourishes, however, in the middle of the palm groves, some two kilometres from the *souq*, and is the more picturesque. Here potters work in an old workshop but now use an electric wheel. They take clay from the *wadi* which is spread on a straw mat and trampled laboriously, to make it smooth and pliable. The potter still shapes large water storage jars which, when thrown, must be kept bound with a cord for a day to prevent them spreading. The pots are then fired in dome-shaped kilns, heated with brushwood, beneath the palm trees. Rows of pots are carefully stacked inside the kiln, one above the other, to reduce breakages.

Jabrin Palace, some dozen kilometres from Bahla, is quite different from Oman's other forts. It never guarded a major settlement and stands today in just a little village. Indeed, originally it guarded nothing at all but was built simply as a residential palace by Bilarub bin Sultan Al

Yaarubi in the 1670s. The two great gun towers at diagonally opposite corners of the building were added later and gave it considerable strength.

This huge palace was built for an elegant and civilised lifestyle: its high-ceilinged rooms are well proportioned and five of them have beautifully painted ceilings. Niches in the walls held lamps and ornaments — today they have been furnished with Chinese porcelain, copper bowls, glazed pottery and oil lamps, as they must have been in the past. The palace boasted a library, and on the roof was a mosque with exquisite ceiling and a Koranic school-room. The main staircase has poetry inscribed in the plaster of its domed roof.

The palace has two small courtyards, virtually adjoining each other, which indicate that the building was originally conceived in two separate blocks, later joined together. A *falaj* flowed right through the palace, as in most of Oman's forts, and there were also a couple of wells as a

The great fort of Jabrin is the most elegant in Oman.

A fine painted ceiling in Jabrin fort.

Rustaq's fort is perhaps the oldest in the land, first built by the Persians before Islam.

precautionary measure. Security was provided too by a number of secret passages and stairways to allow the Imam to make a rapid exit, or his guards to effect a surprise entrance into the main public rooms. The tomb of the founder is set in the lower levels of the palace with an inscription above bearing the date 1086 AH. The palace has been beautifully renovated and is certainly worth the detour, as the French guide books would say.

FORTRESSES NORTH OF THE JEBEL

Just as the great forts to the south of the Jebel controlled access into that mountain stronghold, so too a series of fortresses were built along the northern foot of the mountain, holding the entrances to gorges on that side. These forts can now easily be visited thanks to a loop road heading inland from the coastal town of Barka and returning to the coast near Suwayq.

Nakhl is the first of the northern fortresses, set a little back from the road towards the mountains behind it. This village is the centre of the Yaaruba tribe who were the first Arab tribe to come from Yemen and later built many of the country's finest fortresses. Nakhl was their original stronghold, probably built before the coming of Islam; it was extensively renovated in 1989. Beyond Nakhl the road runs along a major *wadi* system with gardens and palm groves the length of the *wadi*. After some 50 kilometres it reaches the outskirts of the vast palm groves of Rustaq oasis.

Rustaq is the major town to the north of the mountains and was sometimes capital of the country under both the

Yaaruba and Al Bu Said dynasties. Even as recently as 1954 the Imam was elected here. Of all the famous mountain towns, Rustaq has preserved the least of its traditional atmosphere. Most of the town now consists of modern houses and the only traces left of old mud-brick ones are close behind the fort.

In the centre of the town, by the *wadi*, however, the great fort and covered *souq* stand side by side. This fort, Qala'at Al Kesra, has one of the longest histories of any fort in Oman since it is thought to have been first built by the Persians in about 600 AD. The oldest tower in the fort is said to date from this period, but the great bulk of the fort itself has been added to and rebuilt a number of times. The present fort is the result of a rebuilding early in the 18th century at about the time when the neighbouring fort of Hazm was built.

Rustaq fort was completely renovated in 1985. It is an absolute maze of passages, staircases and rooms all at different levels. Through the middle of the fort runs a *falaj*, with a light well above it. There are four towers of which one is particularly huge and oval in shape. Two of the towers have cannon platforms, their line of fire dominating the whole oasis. High up on the roof of the fort are tombs of previous Imams, including that of Ahmad bin Said Al Bu Said, founder of the present dynasty, who was buried close by in 1783.

Three of the living-rooms high up in the fort have painted ceilings though not of the quality of those of Jabrin. These ceilings have simple geometric motifs of white on brown, giving them an almost African feel.

Right beside the fort, on the edge of the *wadi*, is a covered *souq* with three parallel alleys fronted with small shops. It has a rather sleepy feel, with few of the shops open at any one time. The whole *souq* can be closed by large metal doors in the middle of the outer walk. Across

A delightful vista of Rustaq's old town nestled in among lush palm groves, framed by one of the fort's windows.

the *wadi* from the *souq* new shops sell modern goods, plastic bowls and buckets and bicycles.

There is a natural hot spring at Kasfah, near the entrance to Rustaq town, to the right of the main road after the roundabout. A kilometre or so along the track is the little village of Kasfah with its modern mosque, hot spring and old watchtower standing side by side. The hot water wells up from deep pits, one of which has now been walled in and tiled around the edge with brown glazed tiles. The water is then led through a white tiled *falaj* to wash places further downstream.

Hazm is a small village some 15 kilometres north of Rustaq. Its large solid fort seems out of place on the open plain here, in a situation with no obvious strategic advantages. The fort, however, is of extremely strong and simple design, an oblong block with huge round gun towers at two diagonally opposite corners. It is of a classic design for cannon warfare and proved its efficacy when the Yaaruba defenders of the fort withstood a nine-month siege in 1869-70, before finally capitulating to Ibrahim bin Qais Al Bu Said.

The fort was built by the Yaaruba Imam Sultan bin Saif in 1708 AD. The date is inscribed on the massive wooden door, beautifully carved at Surat in India, which is the main entrance. Other fine carving appears on doors between passages inside the building.

Before renovation, Hazm fort's blackened passageways and derelict rooms were redolent of the atmosphere of intrigue and strife of centuries past. Arched corridors run around a central light well courtyard and open on to narrow staircases leading down to dungeons (the fort seems to have a surprising number of these) or into darkened rooms where bats whirled around in the twilight when disturbed. Behind the rooms, with their sculpted lime plaster vaulted ceilings are hole-in-the-floor latrines. Here and there a secret staircase gives promise of a quick retreat. An underground passage, many kilometres long, is said to lead to the next village.

The fort is supplied with numerous wells, one of which, disconcertingly, is dug down in the middle of a passageway, and a *falaj* runs under the centre of it. At the corners of the building are two huge towers supporting the gun platforms. A number of fine Portuguese and Spanish cannon still lie in place in the circular gun rooms whose arched roofs are supported by thick central columns decorated with relief carvings. Below the gun levels are a date storeroom and a dungeon. A wide stairway leads to the roof where there is a large drinking trough for horses.

These great forts of the interior either have been, or are being, renovated by the Ministry of National Heritage and Culture. Readily accessible, they are now one of Oman's major tourist attractions.

Cannon platform in the great tower of Rustaq fort.

The strong door guarding the entrance to Hazm fort.

Chapter 6

GATEWAY TO THE WEST

"Al-Buraimi has always been regarded by the Arabs as commanding the road from Al Hasar and the Nejd."
S B Miles, 1919

The Buraimi oasis has always had a strategic importance quite out of proportion to the size of its settlements. It lies at the junction of major caravan routes from Oman, one coming from the east coast along the Wadi Jizzi, another from the south via Nizwa, Bahla and Ibri. Westwards from Buraimi the routes ran on to the towns of the Gulf coast and beyond into Saudi Arabia.

Here at the foot of the mountains a generous aquifer was channelled through the gap between Jebel Hafit and Jebel Aqlah, the *aflaj* were built in ancient times to supplement supplies from the wells, and extensive date gardens were planted. Nine villages shared this fertile oasis: three of them are today in Omani territory and six belong to Abu Dhabi. The Omani villages of Buraimi, Hamasah and Saarah have now all but fused together. They are scarcely less cut off from the other six villages, melded into the conurbation of Al Ain, since the frontier between them is open and virtually unmarked.

The oasis has been inhabited for 5,000 years or more, as revealed by the hundreds of ancient tombs clustered around Jebel Hafit and Jebel Aqlah. In ancient times the inhabitants cultivated the land, and prospered thanks to their position on the copper route between the mines in the Wadi Jizzi and the Gulf ports.

Prosperity, however, can attract predators; the people always had to look to their own defence. A 5,000-year-old village at Hili in the Buraimi oasis was guarded by a number of watchtowers; in recent centuries Buraimi village itself has been defended by a strong fort. Among the guns of this fort is a brass cannon bearing the name 'Said bin Sultan' and the date 1842. It was one of 20 procured at the time from America by the Sultan (see Chapter 2). This

The majestic landscape of Buraimi entices travellers into the interior of Oman.

The main entrance to Buraimi fort.

fort was restored in the 1980s and stands in impressive splendour, near the *souq* and another crumbling old fort once used by the Wali.

The village came to worldwide attention in 1952 when it was occupied by a force from Saudi Arabia, who claimed the oasis as theirs, and were only driven out three years later. This was but the last round, however, in a struggle for possession which went back to 1800, when the Wahhabis from Arabia first occupied the oasis. In the following half century it changed hands numerous times. Buraimi was the kind of place which, as Ian Skeet put it,, "If you happen to be the strongest, you will ensure (it) is yours."

Today the oasis is peaceful and prosperous, the dense palm groves a joy to walk through. The old mud-houses have given way to modern, concrete ones, but many still stand half hidden among the palms. The old *souq*, too, has been replaced by a modern one which nevertheless retains the intimate atmosphere of a traditional covered *souq*. Old silver, rugs from Ibri, a few muskets and swords, can all be purchased there, along with plastic bowls, aluminium pans, and a mass of imported goods.

The Omani frontier posts are set several kilometres to the east and south of the oasis, and must be crossed in order to visit it. There is a modern hotel in Buraimi and others on the Abu Dhabi side of the oasis, which can be reached with no further frontier crossing.

A man proudly wears his khanjar in Buraimi .

Families gather for reaping the date harvest near Buraimi.

THE IBRI AREA

The road south from Buraimi to Ibri crosses a short stretch of UAE territory at the eastern foot of Jebel Hafit, before re-entering Omani territory after Mazyad. Ibri lies some 140 kilometres south of Buraimi; it is the main town of the Dhahira district and is today a quiet little market town, set back a bit from the main road. Oddly, in the 1960s, Ibri was a headquarters for the Petroleum Development Oman oil company and boasted an international airport.

In the centre of the old district of the town the narrow lanes of a covered *souq* stand close beside a dilapidated fort. Behind the fort are the abandoned mud-built houses of the original town. The square beside the fort is alive with people at market time, the women wearing the same face masks as are worn in the UAE, the inhabitants here being Sunni Muslims.

Ibri is still a centre for old crafts which are rarely seen elsewhere. In the *souq* fine red and black striped rugs are sold. These are woven on ground looms by men of the shepherd tribes who roam the hills around Ibri. There are also still a few indigo dyers in the town, who dye the blue-black lengths of cloth which women make into dresses, veils and face masks.

The route from Ibri along the Wadi Hawasina to the Batinah coast is scheduled to be asphalted, thus completing a circuit of roads around the Jebel Akhdar. A little way along this route from Ibri are the remains of one of the oldest settlements in Oman, the 4,500-year-old village of Bat near Dariz. This settlement, which has been well excavated, was protected in the past by strong watchtowers, just as settlements in Oman continued to be until the middle of this century. A huge ancient cemetery of domed, stone-built tombs stands close by the old watchtowers. The hills are lined with further burial mounds.

However, it is a village on the Nizwa road, just to the south of Ibri, which most dramatically illustrates the disturbed past of this region. The old village of Sulaif huddles behind its walls and towers on a rocky outcrop beside a *wadi* to the west of the road. The town walls and towers are still intact, but within, all is deserted and destroyed. Between the ruined mud-houses the lanes of solid rock are polished by centuries of wear.

Fresh crops are prepared in bundles at Ibri market.

The old fortified village of Sulaif on its rocky knoll.

A third-millennium watchtower in Bat.

From the fortified gatehouse of the town, steps lead down on one side to a *falaj*, and on the other to the old arcaded *souq*. The guard at the gate points out numerous inscriptions in the entrance, cut in stone, in plaster or in wood, each one a record of a war or battle of the past. For centuries the inhabitants resisted this strife, until they were finally evicted during the disturbances of the Jebel Akhdar rebellion in 1954. Today a new village has sprung up outside the walls, but it is a pale shadow of the tight building and defiant defences of the old town.

Chapter 7

SOUTH OF THE JEBEL

"To catch an occasional beam of the sun above the trees they (the houses) are usually very lofty."
James Wellsted, 1837

The Semail gap is the only substantial break in the mountain chain, apart from the narrow, winding Wadi Jizzi in the north. The broad Wadi Semail runs for 160 kilometres through a natural break in the mountains, between the limestone bulk of the Jebel Akhdar to the west and the volcanic peaks of the eastern Hajar to the south-east. Pools of water and running streams enliven the stony grey *wadi* floor, lined along its banks with palm groves and dozens of little villages. This fertile, accessible *wadi* was always a key route, the link between the mountains and the coast.

Control of the *wadi* was of vital importance and was secured by the forts of Semail and Bidbid, and the fortified village of Fanja. This village stands on a rocky ridge near the main road. The cliff-like sides of the ridge gave good protection which was strengthened by a continuous wall around the village. This was topped by watchtowers

Above: Schoolgirls head homeward in east Hajar.
Left: Little streams water the palms of the strategic Wadi Semail.

63

A small wicket gate in the entrance door of Bidbid fort.

on higher ground at either end. Today the modern village fills the ground between the rock ridge and the road and *wadi*, and a pottery shop stands by the roadside, next to a flowing *falaj*.

Further inland Bidbid was a key stronghold, with an attractive fort which has been well renovated. It guards two routes into the interior, for the road to the south-east branches off here. This route, through the narrow, twisting Wadi Aqq, was tough and vulnerable in the past; today it is asphalted all the way to Sur.

Beyond the Wadi Aqq a pleasant wide plain, dotted with rugged hills and acacia trees, lies to the south of the mountain range. It is a region which has been inhabited since the earliest times. Thousands of ancient burial mounds, some going back more than 5,000 years, dot the ridges to the south, witness to man's early endeavours here. And across the plain run lines of little craters, access shafts to the dozens of *aflaj* which nourish the palm groves.

In this region one can best savour the atmosphere of traditional Oman, as it was before the days of oil. Here there are a number of small towns which have prospered over the past few centuries thanks to trade with Africa and Zanzibar, coming through the ports of Sur and Al Askhara. Fine houses and forts were built in traditional style, and many of them still stand today though ever fewer are inhabited.

A clear wadi in east Hajar provides cool refreshment to a passer-by.

A camping idyll at Wadi Shab, north of Qalhat.

ALONG THE ROAD TO SUR

One of many impressively preserved tower tombs at Al Shir in the Jayla district.

Ibra is the first oasis along the road, its palm groves protected by a ring of seven watchtowers on neighbouring hills. It is one of the oldest towns in the district for the Harth tribe were recorded in Ibra as early as the eighth century AD. Today the new town is strung along the roadside but to the south of it lies the old mud-brick town, its elegant houses the product of the East African trade, its old *souq* still intact but deserted.

"The houses are decorated with arches and ornate windows. Set into the ceiling of one half-ruined house is a fine collection of Chinese porcelain plates; another bears a date in the year 1778 AD. The houses are usually very lofty. The windows and doors have the Saracenic arch, and every part of the building is profusely decorated with ornaments of stucco in bas-relief, some in very good taste", wrote James Wellsted who visited the town in 1836.

The old *souq* of Ibra still stands intact, though only one shop is now open. Between the small shops is a pleasantly shaded street, its roof supported on thick columns. This was a *souq* for shoppers who came on foot, a total contrast to the modern shops by the roadside, catering for the motor trade.

Deep in the mountains to the east of Ibra is one of Oman's most extraordinary archaeological sites. High above the Wadi Tayyin, an almost vertical cliff of rock rises from the plain. There on a very high range, at Al Shir in the Jayla district, stand the remains of some 90 tower tombs, built more than 4,000 years ago. The highest still rise to about eight metres, their dry-stone walls in perfect condition today. Tombs of the same period, the third millennium BC, are found in Bat, Muscat and other parts of Oman and the UAE; they were built of stone, as high as a man or a bit higher, but never as soaring towers like the Al Shir ones. The daunting drive up the cliff face, and the extraordinary antiquity of these great towers, makes this a most exciting place to visit.

About 20 kilometres beyond Ibra, and a little to the north of the road, is the village of Mudairib. Today this gives the impression of being the oldest, most splendidly traditional village in the region, for it is well preserved, perhaps because it is a little away from the road. In fact, however, it is one of the more recent villages; members of the Harth tribe moved here and built the place in the 18th century AD.

Mudairib is defended by watchtowers set on a couple of hills on the north side, and by tall fortified buildings in the hollow beside the *souq*. This must be one of the most attractive *souqs* in Oman, a tree-shaded square surrounded by intact, arcaded rows of shops. In the afternoon, groups

Fortunately, the main road usually by-passes these old centres and the new districts have been built by the roadside, leaving the old towns intact even if partly abandoned. New concrete buildings now form the larger districts, but one can still walk among mud-brick houses and palm groves, along sandy lanes beside open *aflaj* which are the life blood of the towns. And above the buildings, old watchtowers still brood on their steep rocky outcrops.

of men and boys sit around and converse there, in the shady shopfronts or under the trees. Beneath one of the trees a couple of men plait a length of rope. Beneath another, a man cuts up huge fish for sale.

A *falaj* runs under the *souq* with a flight of steps down to it in the centre of the square. Beyond the *souq*, the *falaj* surfaces and runs stream-like alongside the track through the palm groves. In the past, payment for shares in the *falaj* waters helped fund the building of a mosque in Zanzibar. The ties with that colony were close and many of the older men in the village have spent part of their lives there.

When the menfolk of the village are not gathered in the *souq*, they may spend their time in the *sabla*, or meeting house of their section of the tribe. In Mudairib the *sablas* are some of the best buildings of the village, often semi-fortified and with fine wooden doors.

Soon after the Harth had established the village of Mudairib they moved a few kilometres eastwards and built Qabil, whose *falaj* was dug in 1758 AD. Just before you reach this village, the Qabil resthouse stands by the roadside, a good place to stop and break your journey. Some striking modern villas have been built along this stretch of the road too.

Qabil became the seat of the sheikh of the powerful Harth tribe and his abandoned fort still stands in the middle of the village. For a century the Harth supported the Imam against the Sultan and in 1895 their sheikh, Salih bin Ali, led an attack on Muttrah and Muscat and temporarily took both. Twenty years later his son, Isa bin Salih again attacked Muscat but finally came to terms with the Sultan at the signing of the Treaty of Seeb in 1920. However, the Harth again supported the Imam in the 1955 Jebel rebellion.

At the junction of the roads to Sur and Beni Bu Ali stands the attractive little town of Kamil. The old town walls still survive here, and within them are some very fine high mud-brick houses, standing among palm groves through which run the clear waters of a *falaj*. The town is also protected by surrounding watchtowers.

The 20-kilometre journey from Kamil to Bilad Beni Bu Ali is one which until recent times foreigners would have hesitated to make. Ian Skeet wrote in 1970 that no Europeans were safe in the territory, though the traveller Bertram Thomas was well received there in the 1920s. Today the people of the town are as welcoming and friendly as Omanis are throughout the land.

In fact the Beni Bu Ali had reason to be suspicious of outsiders. Unlike their neighbours, they are a Wahhabi

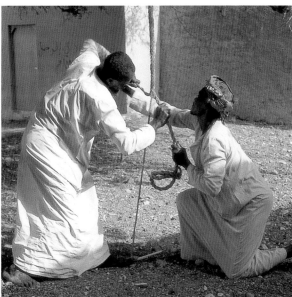

Scenes from Mudairib souq. Top: men cut up fish to sell; middle: plaiting a rope hanging from a tree; bottom: a shady resting place for an afternoon's conversation.

Mudaibi's old souq has been supplanted by modern shops.

tribe, which sometimes led to strife in the past. Their major struggle, however, came early in the 19th century. In 1820 they rebelled against the Sultan, and also murdered a British sailor at Sur. Then they roundly defeated a joint expedition sent against them by the Sultan and the British, killing 300 of their opponents. The following year the British sent a larger expedition, and destroyed the town of Bilad Beni Bu Ali; it was, however, soon rebuilt with British subsidies.

Like all the towns of the area, there is now a large new district in Bilad Beni Bu Ali. Beyond it however, on rising ground, is the old centre with an impressive fort and a magnificent and unique large old mosque. Both this large mosque and a small mosque in the fort's courtyard have

unusual small domes rising to little points. The main mosque is constructed with a series of parallel barrel vaults which terminate in the domes at either end. It has now been carefully renovated.

ALONG THE NEW ROADS

Where the Wadi Aqq emerges to the plain a new road branches off to the right, the road along the Wadi Samad down to Al Mudaibi. Wadi Samad is a broad, fertile *wadi* which was a centre of population even in the most ancient times. Copper was mined in the hillsides there over 4,000 years ago, and from then on the *wadi* was continuously

pulling themselves along under the bridges where the path passes overhead. The mud-brick houses are grouped around the *falaj*, divided by narrow sandy lanes. The old *souq*, along the side of the *wadi*, has however, succumbed to competition from modern shops built opposite, and there is an extensive modern town outside the old walls. Although old Mudaibi gives a good impression of a traditional town, it may be of relatively recent origin, for it is not mentioned in the old histories.

Beyond Mudaibi the road runs south to Sanaw from which another asphalted road runs north again to join the main Nizwa road at Birkat Al Mauz. The whole of this region is peppered with ancient burial mounds, the series of random bumps along every ridge looking as though the land had a bad case of measles.

Some 60 kilometres south of Birkat Al Mauz, on the highway to Salalah, the town of Adam stands as the last outpost of civilisation before the desert sets its iron grip on the land. The large oasis of Adam spreads its palm trees along the foot of the last range of hills south of the mountains. It is protected by a fort and watered by a

inhabited, as the large number of archaeological sites now being excavated there have shown.

Some 50 kilometres along this road is the fine old walled town of Mudaibi. The plain to the north of the town is criss-crossed with lines of *aflaj* and just outside the town walls is a large pond. The *wadi* runs right through the old town, serving as the main street; as a result the town walls are pierced with a series of low arches across the *wadi* at either end, to allow flood water to pass. The strong town gate stands just to the side of the *wadi*.

The old town of Mudaibi is still inhabited and the *falaj* which runs through it is a centre of activity. Women do their washing there, and children swim in the stream,

A young girl of the interior shyly approaches.

Old mud houses of Adam among the palm groves; their gardens are sunk below them to make irrigation easier.

The fort of Bidbid in the Wadi Semail.

A sundial clock for the falaj of Adam. When the shadow touches one peg a farmer opens his sluices; when it reaches the next he closes them.

falaj whose workings are controlled by an ingenious sundial clock. Beyond the new suburbs, at the entrance to the old town, a single pole stands in an open square; set in the ground all around it are small metal pegs. When the shadow of the pole reaches a given peg its owner may open his sluices; when it reaches the next peg he must close them.

Beyond the *falaj* clock the old town winds in among the palm trees. Raised mud pathways lead from house to house, around the sunken palm plots. Beautiful archways are a characteristic of houses and walls here. When James Morris drove past Adam in 1955, on an epic journey across the desert with Sultan Said, he found the town surrounded by high walls and towers, the inhabitants skulking within, and remarked that only three other Europeans had set foot there before him.

Adam's main claim to fame, however, is as the cradle of the ruling Al Bu Said family. The founder of the dynasty, Ahmad bin Said Al Bu Said, was born there early in the 18th century. He was from an ordinary family but came to fame as *wali* (governor) of Sohar and conqueror of the Persians who were attacking the coast. He drove them from Oman for the last time, and for this achievement in 1749 was elected Imam.

Chapter 8

THE DESERTS' CLAIM TO FAME

*"Beyond, a tawny plain merged into a dusty sky,
and nothing, neither stick nor stone, broke
its drab monotony."*
Wilfred Thesiger, 1959

Most of Oman is desert, yet the history books rarely recall this unimportant two-thirds of the country. Unimportant, that is, until a quarter of a century ago, when suddenly the arrival of the oil companies made the deserts of paramount interest.

The largest part of Oman's desert, running from the Dhahira in the north, down through the Jiddat Al Harasis as far south as Dhofar, does not fulfil the classic idea of a desert at all. It is simply barren land, a vast beige-coloured gravel plain, devoid both of plants and contours. The bedouin who inhabit this inhospitable land are few and far between, their camps not marked by the black tents common in Arabia, but rather consisting of a rough shelter under an acacia tree.

Only in the extreme east, in the Wahiba, and along the western borders with Saudi Arabia, is the landscape enlivened with classic sand dunes. Along the Saudi border Oman's dunes merge into those of the great sand sea of the Rub Al Khali, the Empty Quarter. There, in the south, the ancient lost incense caravan town of Al Ubar was rediscovered in the early 1990s, among the sands at Shisr. There too is the sinister salt marsh of Umm As Samim, the 'mother of poison'. These dangerous quicksands were crossed in the 1940s by Wilfred Thesiger who wrote: "We moved forward a few feet at a time across the greasy surface. Often our weight broke through the surface crust of salt, and then we waded through black, clinging mud which stung the scratches on our legs."

The desert sands support many shrubs and small plants.

THE WAHIBA SANDS

A young Bedouin of the Wahiba Sands.

The Wahiba is a large, totally enclosed sand sea, separated from the sands of the Empty Quarter by over 200 kilometres of gravel plain. It covers an area of some 8,000 square kilometres, stretching from near Qabil in the north, down to the coast opposite Masirah island in the south. The main road from Qabil to Bilad Beni Bu Ali runs alongside these sands, making them easily accessible.

Recently the Wahiba has been the subject of intensive study by the Royal Geographical Society in cooperation with the Omani authorities. These sands are rather unusual. They consist of long ridges of dunes trending north-south, with open flat valleys between them. It is very easy to drive along the valleys but extremely difficult to cross the dune ridges which rise in short, choppy crests and hollows. The monotony of a sand desert here is broken by the large number of shrubs and small plants which grow on the dunes; the RGS team had expected to find some 30 different plants in the Wahiba and in fact identified over one hundred.

Fine camels are bred in the Wahiba and the bedouin here, as throughout Oman, ride their camels kneeling

The camel is the prized possession of every Bedouin.

behind the hump, a position requiring superb balance. Some larger wild animals also survive in these sands, especially gazelle which roam freely in the southern section. They are protected, and indeed hunting is forbidden throughout Oman.

JIDDAT AL HARASIS

A key road link between Muscat and Salalah was completed in 1982. This impressive road runs for over 1,000 kilometres, for the most part across the desolate wastes of the Jiddat Al Harasis desert. The new road turns left off the Muscat to Nizwa road, just before Nizwa, then runs through hilly country for 50 kilometres to Adam, the last outpost of cultivation, and the last town for over 700 kilometres.

The desert starts at Adam, a bleak flat, almost colourless landscape which appears literally white at midday. It would be a daunting place to cross, without the lifeline of the road. And indeed it was first crossed by vehicle only in 1955, when Sultan Said (accompanied by James Morris) took a week bumping over the stony ground in a truck.

The oryx, now reintroduced into the wild, is thriving.

A young Bedouin mother attired in simple elegance.

Today three rest houses along the road allow travellers to break their journey in comfort. There is a small administrative centre half way along the road, at Haima, with a hospital, a police post, a school and shops.

So routine has the journey become that now the Oman National Transport Company runs a twice daily bus service between Muscat and Salalah. The coach is comfortable and makes two stops for meals and refreshments at rest houses during the 12-hour journey. There is of course also a domestic air service several times a day between Muscat and Salalah; a return fare can cover bus one way and plane the other.

The new administrative centre of Haima caters to the needs of the Harasis, a desert tribe speaking a language akin to those of the *jebel* people of Dhofar. The Harasis are a poor tribe but in recent years a new interest and source of livelihood has come their way: the oryx. By chance, and also because the Harasis protected them, the Jiddat was home to the last known herd of oryx to live in the wild in Arabia. These oryx were killed by hunters from outside the Sultanate in 1972. By then the Arabian oryx was virtually extinct, apart from a few animals in zoos.

With the support of HM Sultan Qaboos a fresh herd of oryx was brought back to Oman from California and settled in the Jiddat. Gradually, as the animals became acclimatised, they were released into the wild, protected by Harasis rangers equipped with radios as well as guns. The project has been a success and by the late 1990s some 300 oryx were living in the wild.

Omani children beside a desert well.

One of the desert oil wells.

OIL AND GAS IN THE DESERTS

Today Oman's barren deserts have become, in a way, the most important areas in the land. Under the deserts has been found the oil which has financed the modernisation of the whole Sultanate.

Oman was the last of the Gulf states to strike oil, but this was not for want of trying. Oil exploration had started as far back as 1924 and was continuing apace in the 1950s, but still without success.

In a personal attempt to push forward the search, Sultan Said granted the concession for Dhofar to archae-ologist Wendell Philips, and built a graded road for oil prospectors across the Dhofar mountains. But prospects looked bleak and in 1954 the Iraq Petroleum Company abandoned their concession in Oman.

Ironically, ten years later, Petroleum Development Oman, of which Shell is a leading shareholder, made a major oil strike at Fahud (due west of Adam), only 400 metres away from a dry well drilled by their predecessors. A pipeline was built from Fahud to Mina Al Fahal on the coast near Muttrah, and the first oil was exported in 1967.

Since that time many other oilfields have been discov-ered in Oman's deserts, and by the 1990s over ninety fields were in production. Perhaps even more significant for the future are the vast quantities of natural gas found in central Oman in 1990. A huge gas pipeline has been laid across the northern Wahiba to the LNG processing plant near Qalhat.

Oman does not have vast reserves of oil, but each time it was thought that "oil must run out in a dozen years or so" more was discovered and now natural gas has been found there too. For over three decades the country has been an oil exporter; production from around 300,000 to 800,000 barrels a day has been sufficient to transform the country completely. An advance into the 20th century was urgently needed; back in 1955, while crossing the Jiddat Al Harasis, James Morris wondered just how long Sultan Said's rule would last if oil were found. The task of taking the country forward had to be that of a younger man, his son, who became Sultan Qaboos.

Seismic surveys for oil leave tell-tale lines across the desert floor.

Chapter 9

DHOFAR, LAND OF INCENSE

*"Dhofar is a great and noble and fine city.
Much white incense is produced here
and I will tell you how it grows."*
Marco Polo, 1285

The flat stony desert only begins to change about 90 kilometres north of Salalah. Strange low hills, either flat-topped or rising to clear-cut points, interrupt the monotony of the plain, and among them stands the substantial settlement and military encampment of Thumrait. Then the road climbs steeply into crumbling grey limestone hills, the *jebel* of Dhofar.

This range of hills, running parallel to the sea, rises about 1,300 metres high and extends for some 180 kilometres by 30 kilometres wide. The top of the *jebel* is an open, rolling plateau, slightly reminiscent of downlands in England. The northern slopes, dropping down to the desert, are as arid as the land below, but the steep southern slopes which face the sea are different from any other area in Oman.

Above: fisherman silhouetted against the setting sun.
Left: the great mosque at Al Balid, near Salalah, was
supported by about 140 columns.

They catch the monsoon rains which fall in profusion from June to September and are clothed in greenery (and cloaked in mist) for half the year. Slopes and *wadis* support dense thickets of mostly deciduous trees, wild cherry, olives, figs and others; a wall of green in the latter half of the year, a tangle of bare grey branches in other months.

THE DHOFARIS

Roaming over the mountains are goats, camels, and small cattle on which the people depend for their livelihood. The cattle especially are central to the livelihood of the *jebel* people who, for much of the year, used to live largely on milk and meat. They cultivated only a few small fields of grain, beans and durra, and for part of the year could pick the wild fruits and olives. But until recent times, when they have had easy access to the markets of Salalah, their diet has been limited.

The Dhofaris themselves are different from most of the tribes in Oman. The mountain people of the Mahra, Qara and Shahara tribes, still speak their own languages, different from each other but akin to the ancient languages of southern Arabia. The large Bait Kathir tribe, who live mostly in the plain, are a typical Arabic-speaking people.

The *jebalis*, or 'mountain folk', were small, slight people. The men dressed only in a length of indigo-dyed cotton wrapped around the waist as a skirt, with one end slung across the shoulder, rather like the plaid of a Scottish clan. Their hair was long, tied back with a leather thong, and they usually carried a weapon. Today only the old men fit this description; the young have grown tall and strong with a better diet, and dress more like the town people. Their womenfolk wear bright coloured clothes and the older ones often have a gold ring in the end of the nose.

REBELLION AND RECONSTRUCTION

Dhofar's connection with Oman has been tenuous over the ages. A thousand years ago Al Muqaddasi considered it the boundary of Oman and it has been loosely subject to Oman's authority periodically ever since. It was in the last century, however, that the links became closer when, on one or two occasions, the Sultan was asked for help. Then, Dhofar finally became bound to Oman, and it now represents one third of Oman's total land area.

In the early part of the 19th century Dhofar was governed by a freebooter named Muhammad bin Aquil, and after his death Sultan Said sent his troops there. For a while

Animals are the mainstay of the economy in Dhofar's mountainous regions.

Small cattle like this are central to the livelihood of the Jebalis who still live largely on milk and meat.

A Jebali dressed in the traditional length of indigo-dyed cotton, adorned by a khanja (Photo: Helen Cairns).

an unusual leader, American by origin, held partial sway. He had been taken by Muhammad's pirates as a boy of ten. The boy became a Muslim and took the name of Abdullah Lorleyd. From 1880 on, however, the Sultan took firm possession of Dhofar to oust another foreign pretender, and his rule was unquestioned. Unquestioned that is until rebellion flared in the *jebel* in 1963, a rebellion fanned by communist support from South Yemen across the border.

The rebellion led to bitter warfare from 1965 to 1975. Determined military action finally prevailed, leaving the Sultan's forces in control of the *jebel*. After the accession to power of Sultan Qaboos great efforts were made to gain military control of the situation and, once that was achieved, to win back the allegiance of the *jebalis*.

A large share of development funds was devoted to Dhofar where rural centres with school, mosque, clinic, shop and police post have been built throughout the *jebel*. The children are collected from outlying villages and camps and taken to school each day, while work has been found for the men in the *firqa* (the armed forces of the *jebel)* and in Salalah. Today's prosperity shows in the contrast in size between the young and the old.

It also shows in the new buildings in the villages. Today there remain rather few of the traditional round houses with low stone walls and a domed roof covered with earth and grass. These houses were dug down a little into the ground and the branches of the roof were supported by a single central tree trunk. There were no windows or chimney so that the interior became intensely smoky when a fire was lit to ward off the cold and damp. Villages of such houses were not fortified, but they were almost invisible. Now, more relaxed, the villagers favour more obtrusive homes made of concrete and corrugated iron.

Top: frankincense resin oozing from a tree branch.
Above: a frankincense burner.

FRANKINCENSE

Although the *jebalis* were extremely poor until very recent years, they had in ancient times known prosperity thanks to one product: frankincense. In Greek and Roman times, and earlier, incense was much sought after for religious purposes in the lands around the Mediterranean. It was burnt on altars and used for embalming: globules of frankincense were found in Pharaoh Tutankhamun's tomb. In the first century AD, Pliny recorded that the Roman Emperor Nero burnt more incense at the funeral of his wife, Poppaea, than Arabia produced in a year. He remarked that the people of south Arabia were the wealthiest in the world.

The frankincense tree, *Boswellia sacra*, now grows only in Dhofar and northern Somalia. The best crop comes from trees on the inland side of the mountains, but

Frankincense trees brought fortune to Dhofar in ancient times.

some frankincense also grows on the plain south of Salalah. The tree itself, it must be admitted, is a disappointment. It is a low, twisted bush-like tree, only two or three metres high, and lacking a central trunk. The prickly branches spread out from near the ground and carry small, crinkly leaves.

When the silvery bark is pared off, drops of white resin ooze from the scar. These drops, known as *luban*, are left on the tree for two weeks to dry into transparent globules which are then collected for export. Marco Polo described the process 700 years ago: "The trees are like small fir trees; they are notched with a knife in several places and from these notches the incense is exuded. Sometimes also it flows from a tree without any notch; that is by reason of the great heat of the sun there." In Roman times the globules were worth their weight in gold but the incense market collapsed in the fourth century AD, when

Christianity spread throughout the Mediterranean and at first did not use incense. Today only a little is collected; it is used for incense, for perfumes and as a chewing gum.

ANCIENT CITIES

Two thousand years ago, however, control of the incense trade was a much-coveted prize. In 24 BC the Romans sent an army under Aelius Gallus to march down through western Arabia to try to corner the incense market. They reached Yemen but were defeated by disease. More effectively, a few decades later, King Ilazz of Shabwa in the Hadramaut sent a group of colonists to establish a port close to the source of the frankincense.

They found the splendid Y-shaped creek of Khor Rori, at the eastern end of the Salalah plain, where the mountains come down to the sea, with a great waterfall flowing

Ruins of Samhuram on a hillock beside Khor Rori, with a sand bar closing the entrance to the creek beyond.

over them after the rains. There, on a rocky bluff between the arms of the creek, they built the city of Samhuram with substantial stone buildings. On the dressed stones of its entrance way they carved seven inscriptions, one of which tells of its founding. This city was excavated between 1952 and 1962 by an American archaeologist, Wendell Phillips. His team found stores for frankincense, a temple, and pieces of Roman pottery and Greek amphorae.

Today there is a sand bar right across the mouth of the creek and the city is a pile of ruins. It was destroyed in the 11th century AD by Persian conquerors who moved the

Carving of a fleur-de-lis design on the capital of a column, Al Balid.

capital to Al Balid, some 25 kilometres to the west. Nowadays Al Balid, on the eastern edge of Salalah town near the Holiday Inn Hotel, is as much a pile of ruins as Samhuram. In the Middle Ages, however, this city then called Dhofar, was a splendid place, visited by some of the world's great travellers.

Al Balid is built on the open beach but was protected by a creek at each end, and a moat joining them on the inland side. The town was 1.6 kilometres long by nearly half a kilometre wide, protected by a wall and towers. It flourished from the early 12th to the 16th century AD. Marco Polo described it in 1285 as "a great and noble and fine city. It stands upon the sea and has a very good haven, so that there is a great traffic of shipping between this and India, and the merchants take hence a great number of Arab horses to that market, making great profit thereby. Much white incense is produced here."

Today piles of blackened stones mark the site, with a few solid octagonal columns now lying on the ground. The columns had carved square capitals, often decorated with a fleur-de-lis design, unlike any other in Oman. The roof of the great mosque, at the western end of the town, was supported by about 140 columns; it was excavated in the 1990s and remains the largest mosque in Dhofar.

Near Khor Rori the water of a silted creek is sweet enough for animals to drink.

A Salalah horse and rider catch the wind as they gallop across the sand, a short distance from the sprawling capital.

THE SALALAH PLAIN

Today the capital of Dhofar is the extensive modern city of Salalah. It is sited on the coast, at the centre of the semi-circular plain enclosed by the mountains of Dhofar. This plain, some 50 kilometres long by 10 kilometres wide, is very fertile and inland of the town are vast green fields of animal fodder, much of which is used in a modern dairy farm. Near the sea magnificent coconut plantations grow among the houses of the town itself. These plantations, with their tall, smooth stemmed trees, grow right down to the water's edge and are the most lasting impression of the city of Salalah. Beneath their high waving fronds bananas, papaya, wheat, millet and sugar cane are grown. Happily the modern development of the town has spread around and among the coconut groves without demolishing them.

Salalah today is a long town spread out beside the coast, its shape perhaps determined by the fact that it absorbed three or four existing villages from the past. The major roads run parallel to the shore among modern buildings, while on the beach stands the rambling palace, now

Mirbat Fort, the site of the last battle of Dhofar's civil war.

renovated and enlarged. This palace was the home of Sultan Said from 1958 until the accession of his son in 1970, a home which he never left for 12 years.

A little inland and to the west of the palace is a district where some of the old houses of Salalah still survive, albeit in dilapidated state. These were once large merchant houses, two or three storeys high, their windows closed by ornate wooden shutters which opened in four sections. On the outside they were plastered and painted in broad bands of white and grey. At the corners of their roof lines were crow-stepped crenellations, reminiscent of houses in central Saudi Arabia. Not far from the old houses a fine, white painted, domed shrine stands in the Bin Afif cemetery, beside a new mosque and a little to the west of the modern *souq*.

To the east of Salalah and at the farthest edge of the plain stands the attractive fishing village of Taqa with some fine old houses. An even more picturesque village is that of Mirbat, beyond the ancient site of Samhuram. Here the last pitched battle of the Dhofar rebellion was fought around the old fort and won by the Sultan's men. The village has many fine houses with carved window frames.

At the other end of the plain, the coast to the west of Salalah curves round to the sheltered bay of Raysut where a modern harbour has been constructed. This is the main port for Dhofar and is also a centre for fishermen who cast their nets for crayfish, lobster, kingfish and sardines. In

Ministry of Agriculture premises in Salalah; it supports the cultivation of crops and the raising of livestock.

the late 1990s, a massive development of the port was undertaken to convert it into a huge container terminal, able to take the biggest container ships (carrying some 6,000 containers each). Raysut, near the busy shipping lanes of the Indian Ocean, will transship containers destined for the Gulf and even for the Indian subcontinent.

The picturesque village of Mirbat provides a gentle skyline to this inlet of water.

Chapter 10

MOUNTAINS OF THE MUSANDAM

"Little villages niched themselves like eagles' nests."
William Palgrave, 1865

The mountains of the Musandam rise straight from the sea. The sheer grey limestone cliffs, at their northernmost point, form the sentry post to the Strait of Hormuz. This gateway to the Gulf has acquired a strategic importance unique in its history over the past few decades, due to the dozens of oil tankers which pass each day through the busy waterway.

At its narrowest point the Strait is a mere 45 kilometres across, the mountains on either side controlling access. The Omanis take seriously their role as custodians of this vital waterway. Despite its remoteness, they have built a good access route to this northerly part of their domain, a vertiginously steep, graded road hacked out across the mountains in 1982 by their army engineers.

The northern tip of the Musandam is almost separated from the rest by two very long inlets cutting into the mountains from either side and leaving an isthmus only two kilometres wide between them. At the northern end of this semi-island is the village of Kumzar, squeezed into a small bay between the cliffs and the sea. The inhabitants have a language of their own, closer to a dialect of Persian than to Arabic.

The main town of the north is Khasab, which stands on a bay near the mouth of the longest creek, the Khor Sham or Elphinstone inlet. Khasab has been considerably developed as a regional centre and has an aerodrome, a hospital, schools and a hotel. It is now linked to the UAE by a scenic asphalt road all along the west coast. On its wide beach the fishing boats are drawn up; behind, dense groves of palm trees fill the bay. These were the two sources of livelihood in the past.

A fishing dhow sets its course north along the craggy Musandam, a natural haven for marine life.

After rainfall the mountain may blossom like a meadow. Here a spiny milk vetch flourishes near the summit.

Some of the Musandam's mountains can now be crossed by graded roads.

MOUNTAIN PEAKS

The great limestone massif of the Musandam is separated from the rest of Oman by a 70-kilometre strip of UAE territory, and from the other limestone ridge of the Jebel Akhdar by a range of volcanic peaks. The mountain people call their home Ru'us Al Jibal, the 'mountain peaks'. The name Musandam means 'the anvil', perhaps because the restless waves constantly pound the base of its cliffs.

The folded layers of grey rock run in clear stripes across the mountains which are dramatically bare of vegetation, except where man, with Herculean effort, has carved a few pathetic fields. Palgrave's description of over a century ago is beautifully evocative: "Now the granite wall went sheer down into the blue ocean; now it spread out into clefts, down which winter torrents ran, and where little villages niched themselves like eagles' nests; close by them patches of green sprinkled the mountain ledges".

These ledges, in fact, were carefully constructed terraces; the boulders of the terrace walls so huge at times that it seems as if they must have been aligned by giants, not men. Crops grown in winter were fed by rain. Every drop of water which fell on the mountains was carefully collected and brought to the fields by little rocky conduits constructed across the hillsides.

Beside the fields, low, flat-roofed stone houses were grouped close together. Each house had a single room, entered by a narrow door in the long wall, with an enclosed terrace beside it providing the main living space. Inside the house was a row of huge storage jars, for water, dates and grain, jars so large they could hardly have been brought through the doorway. The walls and ceiling were often blackened by winter fires.

Outside the house, in the courtyard, a large rock might serve as a bench, its surface polished smooth by generations of mountain folk sitting there. Another rock might have a cup-like hollow which served as a mortar. The courtyard was sometimes decorated with little pictures of men on donkeys or camels, picked out white on the grey black rocks. The villages were only slightly fortified with an occasional defensive tower in some of them. So close were they, however, to the colour and structure of the mountains, so precariously perched on vertical cliffs, that even if they could be spotted from a distance, approach was often near impossible.

The people drew their water from large cisterns sunk into the ground. These oblong cisterns were some 20 metres deep, 25 metres long and a metre or two wide. Many still hold water today, a thick, unappetising looking liquid that one might hesitate to drink. An old can hanging from a wooden pole serves to draw up the water. The cistern, like the fields, was fed by a system of little conduits from the slopes above.

A small farm is almost hidden from view among the rocks of a great gorge.

Mountain crests create a dramatically layered backdrop to the Musandam coastline.

A gravestone with a carving of jewellery, high in the mountains of Musandam.

So great an effort must have been made by the inhabitants of these mountains, and for so little reward. Yet the villagers of recent times were heirs to a long tradition in their struggle for survival here. On the ridges above some of the villages are ancient burial mounds, thought to be some 5,000 years old.

Today many of the mountain villages are abandoned, or inhabited only by an aged couple or a family who cannot face the upheaval of following their neighbours down to the coastal towns. Sometimes those who have left may return for a weekend; a padlock on the door of their house keeps everything safe for their return. The villages, inhabited or abandoned, look alike in the mountain fastness. The little fields are rarely cultivated today, but sure signs of people still are the goats which invariably graze the arid slopes near villages where life continues. New metal water tanks by the roadside are another sign of population; these cisterns are filled each week by a government water tanker which crawls painfully up the graded road over the high passes.

The precipitous graded track zigzags in a series of hairpin bends over two high mountains, on its way from Dibba to Khasab. Initially it follows a magnificent gorge running parallel to the coast, then starts the first near-vertical ascent. On the far side it drops down into the vast Wadi Bih, before undertaking an even steeper pass to Khasab. Yet accidents are rarely seen on this track. The sheer drops and vast vistas impress caution on even the most rash of drivers. Along the bed of the Wadi Bih, another track leads down to Ras Al Khaimah, on the west coast of the UAE.

Group of Shihuh men with their yirs or small axes.

THE SHIHUH

The people who have dared to make their home in such inhospitable terrain are the Shihuh tribe, very different from other Omanis. They speak a language of their own which outsiders cannot follow, although it appears to be a mixture of Arabic and Persian. Now and then they produce a blue-eyed fair-haired child in their dark haired families. Until recently they lived an isolated existence in their mountain strongholds, which outsiders rarely dared to penetrate.

They managed to eke a living by seasonal migration down to the seashore in summer. There they gathered the date harvest and lived by fishing. In winter they went back up the mountains to cultivate their fields. Then they could live from the rainfall which filled their cisterns and fed their fields, but a severe drought in the mid-1980s drove many of the remaining people from their eyries.

The Shihuh were always warlike, fighting among themselves when there was no other call on their arms, but always supporting each other against threat from out-side. Their favourite weapon, which they still carry as part of their formal dress, was a small axe on a long han-dle, rather like a tomahawk. It seems an unlikely weapon

A fisherman takes a nap on the shore near Khasab.

Thousands of graves on an empty plain mark the site of a great battle in 11 AH.

but in the hands of the Shihuh could be very effective. The origin of the tribe is a mystery which has intrigued scholars. Were they, perhaps, the original inhabitants of Oman before the Arabs came, and sought refuge in the mountains when their land was overrun.

One of their towns is the port of Dibba, a town divided into three sections of which the northern part, Baya, belongs to Oman. In fact the divisions of this town are not new: Portuguese plans of the 16th century show three separate districts there.

Dibba lies on a large bay enclosed by mountains. Its setting was described by Palgrave: "The Gulf of Debee (is) a magnificent bay, scarcely inferior to that of Naples… behind it circles a panorama of mountains worthy of Sicily." The people make their living from their date palms and from fishing; the little harbours are alive with craft and fishermen pull in their nets on the beach and spread their haul of sardines or anchovies to dry on the sand.

In ancient times Dibba was a prosperous port, the main town of the peninsula. Just after the death of the Prophet Mohammed (PBUH), however, the region revolted and refused to pay the *zakat* tax. The Khalif sent armies to subdue the rebels and in 11 AH (632 AD) a great battle was fought just outside the town. At the end of the day the Khalif's forces were victorious: Islam was secure in Oman.

Some 10,000 men are said to have died that day and the town of Dibba was sacked. Dibba never recovered its former position and has remained a quiet little fishing town ever since. On the plain behind the town a lonely cemetery with thousands of standing stones lies silent beneath the acacia trees, at the foot of the Musandam escarpment. It is the cemetery, men say, of that epic battle long ago.

An old lady of the Shihuh with her granddaughter.

A TURBULENT PAST

"The tribes are perpetually at war with each other."
Ibn Batuta, 1329

Oman has always been a profoundly tribal society. The divisions, rivalries, hostilities and alliances among the tribes are often centuries old and in some cases go back to the earliest days of the country's history, reflecting the different origins of the tribes who came to settle here. But the patterns were never stable; tribes changed allegiances and factions over the ages, and in the past no ruler could ever be certain of where support would lie.

The Omanis, in fact, were never easy to rule. Their own great history book, the *Kashf Al Ghummah*, gives a revealing sketch of their character: "Now the people of Oman are endowed with certain qualities, which it is my hope they may never lose. They are people of soaring ambition and of haughty spirit; they brook not the control of any Sultan, and are quick to resent affront; they yield only to irresistible force, and without ever abandoning their purpose." Their history goes a long way to explain their character; or is it after all their character which determined their history?

PREHISTORIC OMAN

While well-shaped flint tools indicate the presence of man in Oman some 8,000 years ago, it was about 5,000 years ago that he really began to make his mark on the landscape. Throughout the country, with the exception of the most barren desert, strange mounds may dot the skyline of any ridge or hill.

These are ancient burial mounds, the oldest built a little before 3000 BC; some of them are known as beehive

A 5,000-year-old tomb near the village of Bat in northern Oman.

A falaj brings water through an underground tunnel to irrigate the palm groves.

be worked. Traces of very early mine workings have been found by archaeologists there, the visual evidence for a trade previously known only from ancient Mesopotamian clay tablets. These documents were the business records of merchants who brought copper from a place called Magan. The oldest reference to this land was a report of King Sargon of Akkad in the 24th century BC, indicating that he brought ships from Magan to his quays of Akkad. The documents referring to Magan continue for some 600 years, and then they cease.

The records on the ground cease too. The copper mines seem to have been worked in the third millennium BC, then not again for a thousand years; they were opened a third time on a large scale, in the Abbasid period of the ninth and tenth centuries AD. These archaeological discoveries have established that the mystery land of Magan was most likely the Hajar mountains. Settlements of the third millennium have been found at Bat near Ibri, in the Wadi Jizzi and in the Wadi Samad.

By the second mining period, that of the first millennium BC, there were far more settlements and many tombs. By this period, also, we begin to be able to name the people who came to be living there.

EARLY SETTLERS

The first settlers whose name is known today began to appear in the eighth century BC. They were the Yaaruba tribe who had trekked north from Yemen. Their descendants were to play a leading role in Oman's history more than 2,000 years later.

Soon other settlers came into Oman across the narrow sea from Persia, from the sixth century BC onwards. These newcomers brought with them a vital skill, the knowledge of how to make the underground water channels known in Oman as *aflaj*. The Persians were to stay in Oman for some 1,200 years, until the coming of Islam, and by the time they left there were about 10,000 *aflaj* all around the Hajar mountains. These water conduits enabled huge tracts of previously barren land to be cultivated.

In the extreme south of the country, in Dhofar, prosperity at this time came from a different source, from the export of frankincense. Here, too, settlers are recorded as having come from outside, from the Hadramaut, to control the lucrative incense trade.

During this period, from the second century AD onwards, other tribes began to come from Yemen, the Azd. A few centuries later more Arab tribes, from Iraq this time, came down to Oman and settled in the northern part of the country. The Arab tribes began to challenge Persian supremacy.

tombs, from their shape. Burial mounds are common south of the *jebel*, especially north of Sanaw and high burial towers dot the mountain top above Wadi Tayin in the Jayla district. Tombs are also found high up on Jebel Akhdar above Sayq, and out into the fringes of the desert south of Adam, or within a few kilometres of the capital Muscat itself.

There are burial mounds too on the hillsides of the Wadi Jizzi and the Wadi Samad. In both these areas the early inhabitants of Oman found copper, the most valuable metal of the ancient world because it was the first to

The two groups of Arab tribes, northern and southern, reflected the ancient division of the Arabs between Qahtani and Adnani (or Nizari) factions. In recent centuries this ancient split was absorbed into the rivalry between Hinawi and Ghafiri tribes; this rivalry started over the election of an Imam in 1723 and spilled over into violent civil war. Although the division was not absolutely clear-cut, on the whole the Yemeni Qahtani tribes were Hinawi and the northern Adnani tribes were Ghafiri.

In the early days, though, Arabs and Persians shared the land, with the Persians to the north-east of the mountains in Sohar and Rustaq and the Arabs to the south-west. The Awlad Shams tribe was dominant then among the Arabs and their sheikhs became the rulers, with the title of Julanda given to them by the Persians.

When the teachings of Islam were brought to Oman by Amr ibn al As in 9 AH (630 AD) the Julandas were converted. The Persians refused to accept Islam and so they were driven out of Oman by the Julandas. The latter ruled for some two centuries; they and most of their people adopted the Ibadhi faith of Islam and in 751 AD Julanda bin Masud was elected the first Imam. Eventually their grip weakened, however, and they were overthrown at the battle of Majaza in 793 AD.

A copper arrowhead made some 4,000 years ago.

Old forts guarded the vital aflaj and the palm gardens beyond.

Ancient cannons still flank the entrance to Nizwa's great fort.

Old fort in Bat, near Ibri.

TROUBLED TIMES

For many centuries Omanis lived a disturbed life. They cherished the ideal of being ruled by an elected Imam but the rather democratic, elective system could not bring stability to the volatile tribes. During disastrous civil strife in the ninth century AD many of the country's *aflaj* were destroyed. The disturbances, combined with the great prosperity built up in Sohar in the ninth and tenth centuries from trade with the East, inevitably drew outside powers to intervene.

During the early centuries of Islam the Khalifs had frequently tried to bring Oman under their sway. The independent tribesmen resisted. In 892 AD, however, Muhammad bin Nur was sent by the Khalif from Bahrain with an army 25,000 strong to subjugate Oman. He killed the Imam and sent his head to the Khalif, then set about subduing the people; "he cut off the hands and ears, then scooped out the eyes of the nobles, inflicted unheard-of outrages upon the inhabitants, destroyed the water courses, burnt the books, and utterly desolated the country." When he left, the infuriated people rose and killed the deputy he appointed to govern them.

Less than a century later the Persians invaded and sacked the great port of Sohar in 971 AD so that the city never really recovered. Oman was invaded again in 1064, this time by the Turks. Two centuries later the Persians returned and the whole coastline was made subject to the island kingdom of Hormuz.

For much of this period Oman continued to be ruled by Imams, but in the mid-12th century another tribe, the Nabhan, seized power and ruled as *maliks*, kings, for two and a half centuries; and their influence continued beyond that.

PORTUGUESE CONQUESTS

Into the quiet waters of the Gulf of Oman sailed the fleet of the Portuguese commander, Alfonso de Albuquerque, in the year 1507. For the coastal cities of Oman it was a fateful day; they were to be ruled by the Portuguese for almost a century and a half. The Portuguese subdued the prosperous little ports with much brutality, killing all who opposed them and cutting off the ears and noses of prisoners, to make an example to any who dared resist further. They established their main base at Muscat, whose fortifications they greatly strengthened.

The Portuguese commander wrote a detailed account of all he found on the coasts of Oman, an account which is of particular interest since it complements earlier descriptions given by Marco Polo in the 13th century and Ibn Batuta in the 14th century. For some of the towns that he took, however, his description was to be the last. Qalhat never recovered from the destruction he wrought and is now a field of ruins; Qurayyat, which put up the bravest resistance and saw its citizens massacred, is today no more than a fishing village.

The Portuguese did not have long to enjoy their conquests in peace. Other foreign powers smelt profit in the Gulf of Oman. In 1554 the Portuguese fought a sea battle against the encroaching Turks, who attacked and pillaged Muscat in 1550 and again in 1580. One lasting result of the second attack was the construction by the Portuguese of the forts of Merani and Jalali, hastily completed in less than a decade. In 1620 the Portuguese fought a naval encounter against a new rival, the British.

It was, however, the Omanis themselves who were to bring Portuguese control to an end, and in doing so to confirm the supremacy of a new dynasty which was to guide their fortunes for a hundred prosperous years.

THE YAARUBA

In 1624 Nasir Al Yaarubi, a member of the oldest Arab tribe in Oman, was elected Imam in Rustaq. He was determined and energetic; faced with dangerous opponents he soon seized the forts of Rustaq and Nakhl, and then gradually captured the other main towns of the interior. But his aim was to gain the coastal towns too, to remove the Portuguese from his land. Perhaps to this end, in the hopes of winning some outside support, Nasir concluded a trade treaty with the British in 1646, the start of a relationship which was to grow to epic proportions in future centuries.

Nasir's early efforts against the Portuguese in Muscat and Sohar were dispiriting. His forces were rapidly defeated. Then gradually he prevailed, taking first the smaller towns, and eventually, near the end of his life, besieging the Portuguese in Muscat. When plague spread with deprivation inside the town the Portuguese were forced to sue for peace. They relinquished Muttrah and were reduced to the small area within the walls of Muscat. His goal almost achieved, Nasir Al Yaarubi died in 1649.

His successor, Sultan bin Saif Al Yaarubi was of the same mettle and enjoyed an even longer rule. He rapidly drove the Portuguese out, then built up an impressive navy to pursue them from his waters. He used his ships for overseas trade, the only source of prosperity for Oman, and he strengthened his control of the country with the construction of near invulnerable forts such as that of Nizwa. Most important of all, perhaps, he used his wealth to repair the *aflaj*, and even to build some new ones. "Oman revived and prospered; the people rested from their troubles. The Imam himself was humble... he used to traverse the streets without an escort, would sit and talk

Fort Jalali was built to defend Muscat in the 16th century.

Guardian of the abandoned village of Sulaif.

The majority of Oman's watch-towers were impenetrable by the enemy, due to the steep and jagged rock faces.

Muttrah harbour is watched over by this old cannon, long since out of use.

familiarly with the people," wrote the Omani historian, Salil bin Razik.

For another 40 years after his death the country was well governed by his sons and grandson. Peace prevailed and his younger son, Saif bin Sultan, brought wealth to the country by extending the empire in East Africa, taking Mombassa from the Portuguese in 1698.

Some of the best forts in the land were built in this period. Sultan's son Bilarub built the elegant palace of Jabrin, and his grandson, also Sultan bin Saif, built the magnificent great fort of Hazm. But this Sultan died in 1718 leaving only a young boy as his heir, and the country soon slid into civil war. Quick to seize their opportunity, the Persians came back to coastal towns of Oman.

THE AL BU SAID DYNASTY

Fortunately for Oman another worthy leader came to the rescue. Ahmad Al Bu Said, Wali of Sohar, had resisted the Persians' attempts to take the town. He then set about clearing them from the other coastal towns, and by 1748 had succeeded, killing the last of them at a banquet in Barka. He was then elected Imam, the undisputed leader, in the following year. To mend fences with the previous dynasty he married the daughter of one of the last Yaaruba rulers.

Ahmad and his son Said both ruled the country as elected Imams, but Said had little taste for the job and his own son, Hamad, became the effective ruler during his lifetime. Hamad established his capital in Muscat and was known as Sayyid, the start of a long tradition. Only one later Al Bu Said ruler was ever elected Imam. However, other Imams were sometimes elected in the interior, and at times this lead to conflict.

The Al Bu Said rulers continued the outward-looking policies of their predecessors, strengthening the ties with Britain and developing the East African empire. The greatest ruler of the last century, Said bin Sultan, was a boy when his father died, but as soon as he came of age (17 or 18 years) he killed his cousin and assumed power. He was to enjoy the longest rule of all, from 1806 to 1856, and the most prosperous.

Said became more and more attached to his domains in Zanzibar and spent much of the latter part of his life there. He introduced the cultivation of cloves to the island, and they became the most profitable crop. After his death, however, two of his sons fatefully split the empire between them, one taking Zanzibar, the other Oman.

At that time Zanzibar was by far the richer domain; an agreement between the sons was worked out by the British, involving an annual payment from Zanzibar to Muscat. When the son in Zanzibar defaulted, the British

Sohar's fortress was fought over perhaps more than any other in the land.

Government undertook to continue the payment (known as the Canning Award). This did not compensate, however, for the prosperity generated when the empire was intact. Oman sank into poverty and debt, with a succession of less long-lived rulers challenged by the tribes from the interior.

Another dangerous challenge to the Sultan came from the Wahhabis of Arabia who occupied the Buraimi oasis for the first time in 1800, and were evicted from it for the fifth time in 1869. They encroached on the Batinah and threatened Sohar. Small wonder then, that when the same thing happened again this century and the Saudis occupied Buraimi in 1952, Sultan Said collected an army of 8,000 tribesmen at Sohar to march up the Wadi Jizzi to the attack. He was dissuaded by the British, who wished to handle the matter by international arbitration (but when that did not succeed they retook the oasis by force anyway, with the Trucial Oman Scouts and the Sultan's forces).

Disturbances in the interior in the latter part of the last century culminated in several attacks on Muscat by the tribes led by the Al Harth of Ibra. After the last attack in 1915 a negotiated peace between the Sultan and the tribes was signed at Seeb in 1920. They agreed to peace and non-interference between them, and a free passage to the coastal ports was guaranteed to the men of the interior.

Sultan Taimur, who had been obliged to sign this treaty giving virtual independence to the interior, abdi-

cated in 1932, after a 20-year rule, in favour of his son Said. The 22-year-old Sultan Said was left to tackle the problems of an empty treasury, and lack of control over the interior. For two decades, by stringent economies and reasonable relations with the old Imam in the interior, he managed to keep the state on an even keel. But after the death of the Imam in 1954 a new Imam, hostile to the Sultan, was elected. Rebellion flared in the interior, the flames fanned by the Saudis in Buraimi, and led to open warfare between the Sultan's troops, backed by his British allies, and the rebels.

That rebellion was suppressed in 1959 by the storming of the Jebel Akhdar, stronghold of the rebels. However, it was soon followed, from 1963 onwards, by further revolt in the mountains of Dhofar, also encouraged from outside by South Yemen. By the late 1960s, when revenues from oil were beginning to come in but were not obviously being spent on improving the lot of the people, dissatisfaction became widespread in the land. It was in these circumstances that HM Sultan Qaboos assumed power from his father in 1970 and Oman finally entered a new world, the world of the 20th century. Since then progress has been very rapid, Oman has developed as an impressively clean, modern state and Muscat has become a spacious elegant capital. Fortunately for the country, Sultan Qaboos has enjoyed a long and untroubled rule.

Chapter 12

TOURISM IN OMAN

Oman is one of the most exciting countries to visit in Arabia — there is something for everyone. It is an amazing country with wonderful people, and in a day you can both explore some of the country's most fascinating historical monuments and also gain an insight into modern Omani life.

Until very recently tourism was unknown. There were no hotels at all in 1970, and visas were difficult to get. By the mid-1980s, however, Oman boasted a number of luxury hotels which businessmen alone could not fill. In 1987 a cautious welcome was extended to suitable tourist groups, and to individual tourists. Today the government is actively encouraging tourism, and has made it easier for tourists to obtain visas. Tourist visas (required by all EC, US, Japanese and Australian nationals) valid for 21 days can be readily and rapidly obtained (three days maximum) from Omani embassies around the world, while business visas take one day only. Visitors from GCC states can obtain a visa at the border or the airport.

With breathtakingly beautiful mountain scenery, sand dunes, deserts, wadis, ancient forts and enjoying perfect bathing and sailing, Oman is promoted as a distinctive tourist location; an unspoilt environment attracting a growing demand for exclusive holidays. A number of new hotels and other projects have been completed or are still under construction. The emphasis is on 'quality' rather than 'quantity', and the Sultanate has so far avoided the possible disturbing effects of invasions of tourists ignorant of its customs, instead attracting visitors interested in its heritage, history and archaeology.

Throughout the starkly beautiful country there are more than 500 old castles, forts, walled cities and defence towers, where graceful architecture mixes traditional and contemporary styles, breathing a new vitality into the landscape. It is also one of the few places in the world which has frankincense trees. Oman also supports an varied range of native creatures such as the oryx and

One of Oman's stunning monuments at the entrance to Muttrah.

The picturesque Al Bustan Palace Hotel — the ultimate in comfort and luxury.

green turtles — eco-tourism is an added attraction for those who believe in mixing adventure with care for nature. The remote Musandam Peninsula is also fast gaining recognition, offering dramatic diving for experienced and adventurous divers. The annual Muscat Festival is here to stay as one of the largest cultural, heritage, tourist and entertainment events in the Sultanate, whilst the new millennium will witness the start of some major projects, including 'Adventure World', a safari and amusement park in Barka. New discoveries in the Sultanate include the Hotti Cave, close to Nizwa — a fascinating subterranean passage that leads to an underground lake and spectacular rock formations. The future has exciting prospects to offer the visitor to Oman.

HOTELS

Excellent hotels throughout the land and an extensive road system, serve to make a visit to Oman a comfortable as well as an unforgettable experience. The capital area is especially well equipped with first-class hotels, ideally situated for businessmen near the heart of the commercial districts, and for family holidays on or near the beaches. Sparkling swimming pools await the visitor in the middle of the day; in Oman the sun is always shining, the weather always warm to hot. A number of new hotels and other projects have been completed or are still under construction. The present target is to have 10,000 rooms by 2005, with more than 100,000 tourists annually.

HOTELS IN THE CAPITAL

The **Al Bustan Palace Hotel** is undoubtedly the jewel in the crown of Oman's hotels. Receiving accolades in 1999 as the 'World's Best Business Hotel', this luxurious, brass-domed showcase for Oman's distinctive new architecture sits on a perfect bay beneath attractively jagged mountains, and features 200 acres of private beach and lush gardens with ornamental ponds. The Al Bustan is a five-star hotel, boasting immaculate service and excellent facilities. It is exceptionally well equipped for conferences, while its 600-seat Oman Auditorium is the regular venue for major national and international events. The Islamic or Continental-style guest rooms are

Grand Hyatt Regency's Marjan Restaurant – famous for Far Eastern Signature dishes.

spacious and plush. French, Italian, health food and traditional Omani 'under-the-stars' dining options range from excellent to legendary.

The **Grand Hyatt Muscat** is the first international five-star hotel to be built in the last 12 years. Ornate Omani jewellery designs on the building's façade and magnificent stained glass windows are the main features, while individual works of art have been given prominence in the hotel's interior. The Hyatt features several food and beverage outlets in its impressive lobby, as well as a nautically themed bar, a Latin American, and an African nightclub.

The **Gulf Forum Hotel and Resort,** one of Muscat's oldest hotels, is now looking bigger and brighter following the completion of major expansion works to double the number of rooms and increase the number of restaurants. Standing high above the Gulf of Oman, amid 10 acres of fertile gardens, it has commanding views of the dramatic Hajar Mountains, and is a hub of life for both Omanis and expatriates.

Located next to the Ruwi Novotel (see page 108), the **Haffa House Muscat** is the capital's latest luxury hotel, offering cuisine from all four corners of the world.

The **Hotel Inter-Continental Muscat** was the first five-star hotel in the Sultanate, and has been in existence for over 20 years. Set in 35 acres of lush sea front gardens, the hotel building has been praised for its

The newly renovated terrace at the Gulf Forum Hotel.

The coffee shop at the Hotel Mercure Al Falaj.

fascinating internal architecture — the lobby is dominated by an inner atrium packed with plants cascading to a ground-level waterfall. All guest rooms have terraces with either a view of the mountains or the sea. For guests who want that extra personalised service, the hotel offers the third floor Club Inter-Continental. Dining options are various and lavish. A large-scale renovation project was planned for mid-1999 covering all the guest rooms, and providing a state-of-the-art health club.

There were 76 new rooms added to the **Hotel Mercure Al Falaj** in 1995, while the old ones received refurbishment. The multi-purpose, dome-shaped Grand Hall ballroom can seat 1,000. As well as regularly bringing in international entertainment, the Al Falaj has developed some of the best health and sports club facilities in the Gulf.

Laith Howard Johnson is an elegant small hotel overlooking Shatti al Qurum beach. Its nautical theme reflects the illustrious maritime traditions of Oman, and provides a unique ambience for guests. It offers superb standards of service and is ideal for those who appreciate five-star service, whether on business or pleasure.

The **Majan Hotel** in Bowsher is conveniently located between the airport and bustling business centres

Palm gardens of the Muscat Inter-Continental Hotel.

The elegant lobby of the Muscat Holiday Inn.

of Qurum, Ruwi and Muttrah. It organises trips to the interior, including visits to Jebel Akhdar, majestic forts or the azure waters of the Arabian Sea. The hotel underwent expansion in 1999, adding new facilities and extra rooms.

The **Muscat Holiday Inn** is located in Al Khuwair, the heart of the diplomatic area and midway between the Seeb International Airport and the Ruwi business district. It is a few minutes' drive from the Ministries, Natural History Museum, Oman Exhibition Centre and Sultan Qaboos Sports Complex. It caters for both the businessman, with an extensive range of business support services, and the tourist with its sports and leisure facilities, and live entertainment.

In the heart of the city centre overlooking the capital's main business and banking districts, the **Ruwi Novotel** is within walking distance of the souq and 20 kilometres from the airport. Specifically designed for businessmen as well as tourists, its restaurants serve Continental, Indian and Chinese cuisine.

Next to Oman International Exhibition Centre and airport, the **Seeb Novotel** benefits from bright, modern architecture. A fully-equipped Business Centre was completed

The Seeb Novotel manages the Al Inshirah restaurant which combines Omani and European cuisine.

in 1999, while refurbished rooms offer wide balconies and four-star luxury with either mountain or sea views.

The **Sheraton Oman Hotel**, located in the heart of the Ruwi commercial district, strikes a cool pose in its own beautifully landscaped gardens. Impressive interiors combine older Arabian styles with modern-day Muscat. The rooms and suites are impeccably furnished and combine views of the city and mountains. Italian and international cuisine head the dining options. Service throughout is efficient. The refurbished Lounge for Executive Floor guests is dedicated to meeting the demands of the discerning business traveller, providing unique services and amenities within a relaxed ambience.

The newly renovated **Sheraton Qurum** is situated on Qurum Beach. This de luxe hotel has a new Far Eastern restaurant with teppenyaki and sushi bar overlooking the pool and beach.

HOTELS IN THE INTERIOR

Pleasant small motels have been built at a number of sites in the interior. They group single storey bedrooms around a swimming pool and courtyard garden, and offer reasonable meals in agreeably cool restaurants.

The Sohar Beach Hotel is built in a traditonal style.

Roughly 260 kilometres north of Muscat on the verdant Batinah Coast, the **Sohar Beach Hotel** is the ideal place for combined business and leisure breaks. Efficiently managed, the luxury chalets in this top-class hotel are arranged in a crescent around a distinctive central facility in the form of an Omani fort.

Al Sawadi Forum Resort enjoys an exclusive position on one of Oman's unspoilt beaches. It is 40 inutes by car from Seeb International Airport, and a perfect destination for those looking for total relaxation at a coastal getaway. Its Dive Centre can offer one-day dive packages as well as an equipment servicing unit.

The tranquil location of the Al Sawadi Forum Resort.

Nizwa's **Falaj Daris Hotel** (previously called the Nizwa Motel) was the first hotel to be built in Nizwa. It has a relaxed atmosphere and an attractive swimming pool.

The **Nizwa Hotel** is especially popular with weekend visitors from the capital. It is a comfortable place from which to explore the attractions of Nizwa, Bahla, the mountain villages of Al Hamra and Misfa or the historic towns of the Jebel Akhdar region.

The **Khasab Hotel** in the Musandam region is a pleasant hotel, conveniently placed for exploring this fjord-land of Arabia. Boat trips around the spectacular peninsula, and diving and snorkelling trips can all be organised through the hotel.

The **Sur Mercure Hotel** has world-class facilities to complement its traditional Omani hospitality. Each of the well-appointed 108 rooms has a pleasing décor and comfortable furniture. For those seeking more energetic ways to unwind, the hotel offers several recreational facilities, including a swimming pool.

Sur Beach Hotel, built on the beach on the outskirts of Sur, is a popular stopover on the way to the turtle beaches of Ras Al Hadd. Don't miss the relaxing beach barbecue as the sun goes down.

Overlooking the Indian Ocean and set in private grounds with coconut palms and bougainvillea, the **Salalah Holiday Inn** has all the requirements of a tropical resort. It has extensive sports and leisure facilities, and offers discounted packages, particularly during the summer season.

The **Dhofar Hotel**, in the heart of the beautiful city of Salalah, is just a few minutes from the airport and the main commercial area. All 66 rooms and 12 suites are completely furnished with modern facilities.

There are also a number of smaller resthouses and motels on the main tourist routes which make ideal stopovers, such as **Al Qabil Resthouse** on the Sur Road, the **Qitbit Resthouse**, **Al Ghaftain Resthouse** and **Ghaba Resthouse**.

Cool off in the Salalah Holiday Inn pool, or take a stroll along the plam-lined beach.

INDEX

THE AUTHOR

Shirley Kay first came to Oman in 1970. She spent that stirring summer in the beautiful old British Consulate at the foot of Fort Jalali, on the sea front of Muscat's fine bay, and quite fell in love with the country. She was fortunate in managing to travel as far as Salalah in Dhofar, and to the top of the Jebel Akhdar.

In 1985, she returned to the region, to Dubai, and was able to visit the Sultanate frequently. After an absence of 15 years, the immense changes in Oman were particularly noticeable, and she has attempted to chart them in this book. This revised version was printed after an extended stay in 1998.

The Middle East first became home to Shirley Kay, her diplomat husband and their children when they arrived in Shemlan in the Lebanon to study Arabic in 1965. They have sinced lived in half a dozen Arab countries, about which Shirley has written extensively in newspapers, magazines, books and for television.

SELECTED BIBLIOGRAPHY

Albuquerque, A: *The Commentaries*, 1557; trans. 1875, 2nd edition 1964

Costa, Paolo: *Musandam,* 1991

Dintemann, Walter: *Forts of Oman,* 1993

Fiennes, Ranulph: *Where Soldiers Fear to Tread* , 1975 *Atlantis of the Sands,* 1992

Graz, Liesl: *The Omanis, Sentinels of the Gulf,* 1982

Groom, Nigel: *Frankincense and Myrrh,* 1981

Hawley, Donald: *Oman and its Renaissance,* 1977

Ibn Batuta: *The Travels of Ibn Batuta*, trans. 1962

Lorimer, JG: *Gazeteer of the Persian Gulf, Oman and Central Arabia,* 1908–1915

Miles, SB: *The Countries and Tribes of the Persian Gulf,* 1919

Ministry of Information: *Oman,* 1972 Ibid: *Oman, A Seafaring Nation,* 1979

Ministry of National Heritage and Culture: *Journal of Oman Studies*, annual

Morris, James: *Sultan in Oman,* 1957

Palgrave, William: *Narrative of a Year's Journey through Central and Eastern Arabia,* 1866

Phillips, Wendell: *Unknown Oman,* 1966

Polo, Marco: *The Book of Marco Polo, the Venetian,* c.1298, trans. 1965

Severin, Tim: *The Sinbad Voyage,* 1982

Sirhan, Sirha bin: *Kashf al Gummah/Annals of Oman to 1728,* trans EC Ross; Oleander, Cambridge 1984

Skeet, Ian: *Muscat and Oman, the End of an Era,* 1974

Thesiger, Wilfred: *Arabian Sands,* 1959

Vine, Peter: *A Heritage of Oman,* 1995

Ward, P: *Travels in Oman,* 1986

Wellsted, JR: *Travels in Arabia,* 1838

Wilkinson, JC: *Water and Tribal Settlement in South-East Arabia: A Study of the Aflaj of Oman,* 1977

Williamson, A: *Sohar and Omani Seafaring in the Indian Ocean,* 1973

ACKNOWLEDGEMENTS

I should like to thank the HE Abd al Aziz bin Mohamad al Rowas and staff at the Ministry of Information, Muscat, for their support and for enabling me to travel throughout the country.

I am also especially grateful to Brian and Caroline Lees, John Shipman, and Nigel and Gay Harris, my hosts and guides who took me to many of the enchanting and lesser known corners of the land.

THE ARABIAN HERITAGE SERIES

*If you've enjoyed this book you might like to read
some of the other Motivate titles.*

COUNTRY GUIDES

**Bahrain
Island Heritage**
By Shirley Kay

Enchanting Oman
By Shirley Kay

**Kuwait
A New Beginning**
By Gail Seery

Land of the Emirates
By Shirley Kay

**Saudi Arabia
Profile of a Kingdom**
By various authors
and photographers

UAE GUIDES

**Abu Dhabi
Garden City of the Gulf**
By Peter Hellyer and
Ian Fairservice

**Al Ain
Oasis City**
By Peter Hellyer and
Rosalind Buckton

**Fujairah
An Arabian Jewel**
By Peter Hellyer

**Portrait of
Ras Al Khaimah**
By Shirley Kay

**Sharjah
Heritage and Progress**
By Shirley Kay

NATURAL HISTORY

Birds of the Southern Gulf
By Dave Robinson and
Adrian Chapman

**Falconry and Birds
of Prey in the Gulf**
By David Remple and
Christian Goss

Sketchbook Arabia
By Margaret Henderson

The Living Seas
By Frances Dipper and Tony
Woodward

**The Oasis: Al Ain Memoirs
of 'Doctora Latifa'**
By Gertrude Dyck

ARABIAN HERITAGE GUIDES

**Beachcombers' Guide
to the Gulf**
By Tony Woodward

**Off-Road
in Oman**
By Heiner Klein
and Rebecca Brickson

**Off-Road
in the Emirates**
By Dariush Zandi

**Off-Road
in the Emirates 2**
By Dariush Zandi

Off-Road in the Hejaz
By Patrick Pierard and
Patrick Legos

On Course in the Gulf
By Adrian Flaherty

**The Green Guide
to the Emirates**
By Marycke Jongbloed

The Off-Roader's Manual
By Jehanbaz Ali Khan

Further titles are available. For more information visit our website:

booksarabia.com